Asparagus Opera

A Chinese Family in the San Fernando Valley

By Soo-Yin Jue as told to Jack Jue Jr.

ISBN 9798868486975

Notice: The information in this book is true and complete to the best of our knowledge. It is offered without guarantee on the part of the author or the editor. The author and the editor disclaim all liability in connection with the use of this book.

First published 2023

This book is dedicated to my father, San Tong Jue, with honor, respect and love.

INTRODUCTION

I will tell you our story as I have lived it, Jack. It was not a simple matter of knowing the discriminatory laws that affected our family in America, or of the human consequences because of those laws. It was the nature of both in synchronization with changing identities and in internalization deep within one's interior that unleashed destructive powers of culture clash.

As I have witnessed, culture clash is a phenomenon that few transnational families have had the luck to escape. Jue Joe's family in America was no exception. His family absorbed the full impact of inter- and-intragenerational conflicts. Conflicts aggravated by Exclusion Laws of the 19th and 20th centuries aimed against Chinese in America. For the character of culture clash rises full throttle as interior oceans deep within the psyche explode to turn perceptions of reality. This is so for a transnational newcomer who arrives in a foreign land with a single aspiration—to grow a dream—only to encounter opposing forces that require great resilience on the part of the newcomer to overcome those fiercely applied forces. In Jue Joe's case: forces from those who want to decide who can be an American, and who cannot be an American.

Jue Joe's family in America was impacted by such tropes. These convolutions labored upon each member of his family. They were truths that took San Tong Jue, who was the surviving son of Jue Joe, and who had the sole burden of managing the family's survival on multiple fronts, it took him down an abyss with no means of escape. This was uncharted territory for San Tong Jue, as he navigated the Jue family through unknown parables. Yet, the moment that San Tong had landed upon California's good earth—at the age of thirteen—the dark schism that lay between two worlds of thought had been waiting for him. It had been waiting not only for this surviving son of Jue Joe, but for each member of Jue Joe's family who would experience an immigrant's dream from the viewpoint of conflicting angles.

The 1882 Chinese Exclusion Act...

Signed into law by President Chester A. Arthur on May 6, 1882, the Chinese Exclusion Act of 1882 effectively closed the door on Jue Joe's aspirations to become an American citizen. This is because the Exclusion Act suspended Chinese immigration to the USA for ten years and declared that *all* Chinese immigrants were ineligible for Naturalization.

But before I continue my story, let me backtrack for a moment: Four months prior to the Exclusion Act's passage, Jue Joe had asked the elders of The Chinese Six Companies in San Francisco, California, for advice on becoming a U.S. Naturalized citizen. He wanted to become an American citizen and he wanted the consent of elders who managed all immigration matters for Chinese who belonged to The Six Companies.

The Six Companies was, and still is, a Chinatown benevolent association that originally represented four districts with similar spoken dialects in Guangdong Province, China: Kaiping, Enping, Toishan, and Sun Wui. These Districts originated in a southern region of Guangdong Province, China, that is situated between Guangzhou City and the South China Sea—a region that is called the "Pearl River delta."

Here in the Delta, Jue Joe's village of Sum Gong lies within Sun Wui District. Mind you, the name "Sum Gong" is a Cantonese pronunciation. This Village is also called "Sanjiang" in Mandarin. Likewise, the district of Sun Wui is also called "Xinhui" in Mandarin. But I use Cantonese in this story because it is the dialect that I grew up with.

You ask me, "What does the name 'Sum Gong' mean?"

Well, Jack, Sum Gong Village is a flash of time, and dare I say, it's a unique memoir. First and foremost, Sum Gong Village means "Three Rivers" in English. And the Village is surrounded by three rivers in Sun Wui District that envelope this secret hideaway. Sum Gong Village is located 70-miles south of Guangzhou City in Guangdong Province, China, which is the city that was once called "Canton" in the early days of the 19th and 20th centuries.

Here and now, Sun Wui District was the last stand for the last emperor of the Song Dynasty who, with his royal entourage in AD 1279, fled to this ancient backwater to escape Kublai Khan's Mongolian forces seeking to conquer all of China.

I can tell you that Sum Gong Village is ringed by emerald mountains in the shape of gumdrops. And bamboo trees wave softly at you from those conical-shaped, green gumdrops. Stretch your curiosity and hear gong-cries stream from Macao on the Zhuhai Peninsula situated to the east because Macao is close enough for you to touch. Or take a swim in a shimmering river blinded by Sum Gong's brilliant sun; on its coffee waters, a sailing junk glides you swiftly toward Hong Kong. This is because you are only a stones-throw away from that bustling City parked at the edge of the South China Sea.

In Jue Joe's village of Sum Gong, you hear the songs of ancients bend through a mournful breeze. For the Village moves like an eternal clock as sunbeams count the day round rice fields waving in that breeze, and slow-moving oxen are seen pulling their wooden carts down those fields, guided by sun-bronzed hands. This is a flash of time in the memoir of Sum Gong Village, Jack.

From here, folks braved a perilous journey across the Pacific Ocean to grow a dream in America. But because of the effect of Chinese Exclusion Laws in America, they found themselves prostrated before the elders of The Six Companies in San Francisco's Chinatown, seeking the elders' advice and help. This is because the purpose of The Six Companies was to help newcomers from the original four districts of the Pearl River delta find housing, jobs, and it helped them resolve their legal matters too.

And when the heavens tolled for a newcomer's soul, well, The Six Companies in reverence delivered the body home to its respective village for an eternal rest. However, due to increasing violence against Chinese by a segment of the white population in California at the time, which exploded into burnings of Chinese labor camps and lynchings, the elders of The Chinese Six Companies told Jue Joe the following:

"What!? No way! Stay your loyalty with China because white folk greet you with their venom for just being who you are—Chinese. If you cross their shadow they demean and denigrate you, tell you that you can't be an American and they continue to destroy your chances to try to be one…." Blah blah blah.

At once Jue Joe understood that consent from the elders would not fly from their lips.

The 1892 Geary Act…

May 5, 1892, passage of the Geary Act extended the exclusion of Chinese immigrants from becoming U.S. Naturalized citizens. In addition, it required each Chinese immigrant to carry a "Certificate of Residence." This Certificate of Residence effectively labelled Chinese as "foreign" with no American identity. And so, The Chinese Exclusion Act would continue as United States law for another sixty years until its repeal in 1943.

The California Alien Land Law of 1913…

This is the rub, Jack. The California Alien Land Law of 1913 (Webb-Haney Act) forbade aliens ineligible for Naturalization from owning agricultural land, or from long-term leasing of land for more than three years. It was aimed at preventing Chinese and Japanese immigrants from acquiring land to farm, thereby preventing these farmers from becoming a part of an agricultural industry that was dominated by the white community. Moreover, it was advocated by California's Governor Hiram Johnson as a tool to boost his political ambitions.

Shades of alarm, I tell you. For the Alien Land Law would continue to be the law in California until its repeal in 1950 as unconstitutional. However, its impact was extremely toxic and great damage had been done to the lives of immigrant Chinese and Japanese farming families.

You ask me, "How did these Exclusion Laws affect Jue Joe's family in the San Fernando Valley?"

Oh, my dear nephew, they motored our family into a lineup of conditions that made for a perfect storm.

But before I begin our story, Jack, the "Jue" surname is also spelled as Jew, Jiu, Chew, Chiu, Chao, and Chu in Cantonese. It is spelled as Zhao in Mandarin. However, the different Anglo spellings of the Jue surname refer to a single clan, which is identified by the Clan's Chinese calligraphy of 趙 or 赵 in simplified version.

Auntie Soo-Yin, 2023.

CHAPTER 1 – THE BEGINNING

Oh, yes, I do remember…

The night held him captive, strapped to a gurney. An overhead lamp's glare clouded his clarity. Narrowing his eyes, Father pierced that veil for movement that floated around him. But in the emergency room I couldn't help but see that he was rethinking his challenge. A fierce trial stole across his eyes, and I began to realize that he was trying to stay us in his mind. It was as if he held our shadows that danced across his vision tightly with a new kind of urgency—our souls embedded for one last second in the greyness growing throughout his interior. I heard his gasps as he struggled to breathe. I saw beads of sweat slip down his worry. It restyled his countenance, this was clear to me.

In the room I could see that my two older brothers and my three older sisters shared with me the strangeness of Father's crossroad. We tightened like a knot around his gurney. We must have appeared to him damaged as we patrolled in chaotic manner our souls around him. At once Father captured our nervousness: he picked our panic that in his vision grew to cartoon-size. And though his bony limbs lay useless on his gurney, his head flopped unsteadily from side to side as if to blast at us, "No more of this!"

In the room I heard machines bounce with language. Steady wheezes told you that they were breathing and aware of you. I saw a large plastic tube attached to a stainless-steel box pump oxygen down Father's throttle. Another tube snaked skyward from his chest drawing dark fluid into a plastic bag hitched to a pole. Father seemed locked in combat with those two plastic whatnots. He had instructed us not to work him over, and now, he thrashed his head against his pillow trying to jerk these man-made miracles out. But the coils attached to his body demanded a stay on his edge of life.

With all his strength, I tell you, Father lifted his head and shoulders off his gurney to lunge at my siblings and me. But he couldn't take us. Instead, he fell back on his steel slab. No sounds shot from his larynx, but you caught what he meant: "YOU! How could YOU do this to me?" "Let me go!" But we were thinking of ourselves. For this reason we shouted into Father's ears to divert his design: "Dad, remember when…." "It's a beautiful day outside, Dad." "I love you; I truly do." "I'll wait for you in the hallway, Dad...." We didn't know what to do or what to say, you just can't think in that hour.

It was Jack Sr. and Guy, my two older brothers, who seemed to understand Father's meaning: "LET GO OF ME YOU FOOLS!" I could see that my older sisters Joan, Soo-Jan, and Pingileen had not given up. That's four against two if you include me, I thought.

"Lord hear him...," it sang from the heart of Alice, my brother Jack's wife, who spoke swiftly into Father's ears. He was nailed by exhaustion to his gurney, now, and Alice poured into him a prayer, "Lord know him and...." She was a preacher's daughter and she touched Father's interior with the spirit of the high Lord's presence.

Well, I wanted Father to float to sacred heights, but without insight into that place myself, I thought he might, like me, confuse himself along the way. So, I felt relieved to witness this holy fever flowing from Alice. She brought it up and out of her, and this was winging me back to a lost wilderness. For I never knew religion until the day Mrs. Shipman, who was my sister Soo-Jan's piano teacher and whose white hair blasted about like layers of potato chips when she hit piano keys, swore to burn a runt like me.

"Scuttlin' wild on an asparagus ranch with chickens and cats and horse-shit," wailed Mrs. Shipman's pioneer voice. "O child, you be beholden' to the good Lord. Be a fine Christian like me. Now, pray goddamnit!" That day my real confusion began. What if Mrs Shipman is onto something? I thought. What if that oddly lighted place is real up there? I wondered if I might screw the works for Father if I didn't believe. So, as a barnyard stray I began to pray hard.

Suddenly I became aware that Estelle, my brother Guy's wife, had joined us. I also became aware that Richard, my sister Joan's husband, had moved into view. We stood together as a tribe held by the power of one man's final hour. We heard Alice pour the passion of eternal faith into Father and, I like to think, he was floating smoothly through large, passive skies. Yes, cotton skies. Real soft. Then our tear-filled eyes turned to one another slowly in admission of idea, affirming that there was no choice but to pull the tube from Father's throat.

I watched a nurse disengage him. And then it happened. At once Father seemed to relax and to stop his miff with us. He knew there was no escape now. He knew there was no other possibility on Earth but to meet his finality head on. Father impressed upon me the power of his will. He seemed to welcome the mystery of this void, and it was working on him from all directions. But I couldn't sense relief in him of the kind that one is said to gain at this emphatic hour, nor could I feel for myself Mount Olive rising in the room or see the ray of Christ open upon Father's humanity. Instead, I saw an old body wane helpless against white sheets and this frightened me.

From the Emergency room Father was wheeled into a small private room. We trailed behind him like anxious strays. And as dawn spread its smile over the room, there seemed nothing more for Father to do but to wind down his breath as we, too, felt the need to sort out our thoughts in silence.

In this wall-papered room I saw that there was a large bay window, and as the early sun turned through the glass it flared brilliantly on Father's face. The light's intensity chased across his grey, motionless face that used to express so well the joys and sorrows of his life. It was an eerie feeling, but Father looked to me strangely beautiful now.

Jolted from that instant I couldn't believe what came next. With otherworldly strength Father jerked his head hard against his pillow. He drew one sharp, deep breath and I saw his chest arc and freeze in mid-air for what seemed an eternity, then his body sank slowly back in final surrender. That's how Father let go of us.

It was an odd surrender. It was as if he heard an ancient's gong-cry, "When dawn strikes low on the horizon, first orange then pale blue in the eastern sky, have no fear. Look to the East and think of your ancestors. Think of your father with his roots in that village far on the other side of the world. For you are in the lyrics of that ancient spirit. You are part of the sonnets of life, song-like, that roam sonorous across the eastern sky."

CHAPTER 2 – SUM GONG VILLAGE

Standing on Jue Joe's balcony I indulged in the beauty of Sum Gong Village. Scanning the vastness of its farmlands below, I marvelled at Sum Gong's crazy patchwork of human activity, which for a thousand years had crafted itself with impudence onto the Pearl River delta of Guangdong Province, China. Here stood the home in which my father San Tong Jue was born. It was the very home that his father Jue Joe had built in 1903, upon returning from San Fernando Valley's Old West culture in California, to marry and to raise a family of his own on the land of his birth.

Father's Village was no longer a myth to me, the way I had imagined Sum Gong Village to be when I was growing up in Southern California. After Father's passing, I made a pilgrimage across the Pacific to glimpse his childhood dreams, dreams that he had revealed to me in my youth. Sum Gong Village means "Three Rivers," as I'd said before, and is in Sun Wui District near Macao. It holds for me the magic of ancestral lore: the sound of rivers roaring past my soul, the morning flow of emptiness, the mist shrouding mournful secrets—to me that's the feel of Father's ancestral homeland.

I remember it clear: Sum Gong Village is cooking smoke, smells of wet straw and water buffalo, adobe huts arranged in crazy patchwork fashion, and children foraging in spare spaces like strays. This Village is a time warp that somehow defies the years passing by like the rivers perusing through its character.

What gives this Village its whimsy is a kaleidoscope of hump-backed crags. They are ancient mountains that rise to your north and to your east. They leap with the wind in a crash of drums and cymbals when, on New Year's Day, lion dancers wind down their slopes.

Guarding Sum Gong Village is the North Gate, which stands unsparing at the base of Pig's Head Mountain. And there, there atop that Mountain looms a red- and-green tiled pagoda called the "Chan Hong Hop." Up slabs of air the Chan Hong Hop flicks down at you an indelible sight: sunrise and its belly welcomes pilgrims who bring food up stone steps to an altar so that heaven can bestow upon them prosperity and good fortune.

Follow me to a big canal that cleaves Sum Gong Village into equal halves: Hangmei District, which is residential; and Dai Jan District, which is commercial. On the banks of that canal, you catch ancient mangrove trees so thirsty that their thousand-year-old tendrils dredge for existence in the brine-laced waters. Here, you see boatmen pole their way downstream to a market in the next village, each boat filled with baskets laden with goods to sell.

In 1902 villagers saw Grandfather Jue Joe arrive in Sum Gong Village with tall tales of "Gum Saan," meaning gold mountain. They last saw him as a teenager, eager to plant a dream on the other side of the world. "So far away," voiced villagers among themselves, "far from ancient loyalties that bind a people's history in his homeland."

Remember this well, Jack. In 1874 Jue Joe bid farewell to family and friends. He left his kinfolk at the age of seventeen. But in Chinese custom you add one year for time spent in the womb. So, at the age of eighteen Jue Joe wondered if he would ever see his mother and siblings again. For on the far side of the world, invoked his notion, he could only stay their images in his interior. This is how his long journey to America began. Now twenty eight long hard years later in 1902, he had become rich enough to return to Sum Gong Village to marry. He was what the villagers called a "Gum Saan Man" for to the villagers the fabled land of America was truly a gold mountain.

In Sum Gong Village, Jue Joe built a complex of homes for his siblings and himself. He made sure that the exterior of his complex conformed with Chinese traditional architecture. Meaning that exterior wooden doors used chain- and-padlock to keep nogooders at bay. But inside his gray-brick complex, well, California's doors fashioned in the Old-West style with porcelain doorknobs to turn, gave truth to newly acquired tastes.

But he goofed on Fung Shui. The grannies of Sum Gong complained that his front door faced the wrong way. "This is bad luck for us all," gyrated the gullets of grannies. In unison they agreed: Jue Joe had been away far too long to remember Sum Gong's grace and customs. There had to be concession. So, Jue Joe added two side doors to his main house that trended with *fung shui*. And no member of his family ever dared to use the home's front door.

Villagers were eager for news about Gum Saan from this new arrival. And Jue Joe had much to tell them. He had been in scrapes with Lo-Fan laborers who resented his "stealing" jobs from them, and as a result, he sported a scar above his right eyebrow and a crooked little finger. With experiences like this, and there were many that Chinese were experiencing in America, Jue Joe assured villagers that he had become a tough fighter. But truth be told. He still wore a used cotton top and loose trousers and did not blend in with locals on the Western frontier.

One thing was clear, however. Jue Joe did not look like the locals of Sum Gong Village either. He scalped his head of a queue. While the locals still sported long braids, Jue Joe declared his independence from Qing rule, which required that all Chinese males sport a queue as a sign of servitude to Manchu reign.

This act alone was declaration that Jue Joe had morphed into a foreign-local. In midair he twirled his American Colt .44 M1878 six-shooter and test-fired the piece in Sum Gong, showing his stance for acquired independence.

The mothers of Sum Gong noticed one thing about Jue Joe: He wore shoes. Jue Joe's flare for cowboy boots spoke to them of a fabled land. Clearly, this lifted him degrees higher than other suitors who padded round wet fields in their bare feet. And as locals wore conical hats with queues streaming beneath those hats, Jue Joe donned his favorite Stetson.

For this treason, believed mothers of Sum Gong Village, the scalping was proof that Jue Joe's character vibrated with high valor and fearless moves. The conclusion that matchmakers drew in Sum Gong Village rested with giggles, winks, and fluttering of eyelashes for this old-but-fresh new prey.

But truth be told. Jue Joe was no longer a young man. His face flashed at you a walnut; feral squiggles lay bare that truth. Still, he had a pleasing appearance. He had a high straight nose, a stubborn square jaw, lips cut straight as a bullet, and he was taller than most of the Chinese men of Sum Gong Village.

"But Soong!" exclaimed farmers to Jue Joe as he passed by their fields. They addressed this kinsman by his Chinese birthname with emphasis on the first syllable of "But," for Jue Joe was suspected of having forgotten its worth, having steered through many foreign seas.

"But" was Jue Joe's generational name that conveyed his position in a Song Dynasty's poem. The Poem was penned by its second emperor Zhao Guangyi who was called "Emperor Taizong" and who was the direct ancestor of Jue Joe. This generational poem defined how many generations a clansman was from Emperor Taizong, and it defined Jue Joe's obligations within the Jue clan for all eternity.

In Sum Gong Village the matchmakers believed that Jue Joe was flush with cash. Yes that. He had built a new two-story house of bricks coated gray as a bank's vault. Ten miles north of Sum Gong Village the pig traders in Ma Choong Village thought so too. They had heard of Jue Joe's tales of Gum Saan at an open market.

So, of young girls in Ma Choong Village who herded hogs to a river and who hawked them for barter, seventeen-year-old Leong Shee was handpicked to be Jue Joe's bride. In 1902 she was nailed because at seventeen-years old, Leong Shee would soon be eighteen and, of course, would be passed her prime to pump for a hefty dowry. Her family of "Leong" was in desperate need; they were poor as squirrely mice and Leong Shee was the only daughter out of five sons of Widow Leong. The girl had to be hitched and who better than to a Gold Mountain man?

"You'll get a water buffalo and nothin' more," upped Jue Joe's craw. He anteed the Widow Leong who'd lobbed her price like kumquats up and down his character. Across a small table she perched, her larynx vibrating, astounded by the man's impudence.

"...and, and my daughter Leong Shee," injected Widow Leong, "she has the strength of two water buffalos. Two! And she can plow a straight line down a rice field. What's more, she can hawk your sweet potatoes and drum for money at the market square. YOU owe me better, my good man."

The late afternoon pounced its dim bars of light down the distress of a worn woman. Squinting at this foreign-local who threw a hammer-and-scissor poke, Widow Leong's interior grasped that her village-style melodies would only win her cold defeat.

So, courage corkscrewed out the Widow's mouth, she blurted, "My daughter Leong Shee is worth *three* cows and *four* pigs! But, alas, it is impolite to challenge a man. You shall have her as you wish."

Poor poor Leong Shee. Her sobs barreled through Jue Joe's two-story house in Sum Gong Village. It was her wedding night and washed with tears, she barely made out a Colt .44 hooked in its leather holster; it hung like a noose from Jue Joe's western-styled bedpost. The smells of Mexican tobacco and whiskey assaulted her nostrils, too, and pinned atop this wedding bed, Leong Shee felt a groom's hands till her fields.

Scared out of her wits, but in accordance with wifely duty, Leong Shee delivered to Jue Joe his first-born son—San You. The year was 1903. At once Jue Joe entered San You's name onto an altar in the Clan's ancestral hall in Sum Gong Village called the "Cheung Kwong Hong." Two years later Leong Shee delivered to Jue Joe a second son—San Tong, who was born in 1905. San Tong's name was given a tablet, too, and was positioned to rest on the same altar for all eternity; his soul imbedded forever on rows descending from Emperor Taizong, or Zhao Guangyi which is his birthname in Mandarin.

But I confess, Jack, life's rhythms are peculiar. Fortunes appear; fortunes vanish.

Jue Joe's fate was no exception. Overnight his remittances from younger brother Jue Shee in Los Angeles had stopped without explanation. Around the turn of the century, Jue Joe had helped his brother emigrate to Los Angeles. Jue Shee was fifteen years his junior and he was to continue the family's business that Jue Joe had struggled years to build. This was a kid brother's job. Jue Shee was instructed to send Jue Joe money in Sum Gong, as the latter had returned to the ancestral village to raise a family of his own.

And now, now relatives in Sum Gong threw their chins up. Their eyes squared down on a kin's empty cash flow. Remittances had lifted Jue Joe's family above the ordinary in Sum Gong Village, but in a toady, Gum Saan and prestige that such connection had brought to them pranced into oblivion. On this vision Jue Joe's relatives rolled their chins downward in despair. They flicked their lips up in air and words glazed the clouds with unintelligible feelings. For the Jue clan had fought centuries of no tomorrows in China's long and thunderous history, wagged their tongues at Jue Joe. And through each of those rumbles, continued his kinfolk, the Clan had survived victorious. What's to become of us now? relayed tongues among themselves. Their gong-cries grew to bed lam.

As a result, Jue Joe did what a guy might do today. He did what a guy might do tomorrow. He left Leong Shee to face her fate. He took passage on the SS Mongolia that scuddled him to the rim of the San Francisco Bay. From there, he wound his way to Los Angeles to hunt down that varmint of a kid brother Jue Shee. Why such impudence from a squirt? queried Jue Joe to himself. This enigma motored through his interior.

I confess, without Jue Joe in Sum Gong Village—Leong Shee's real life began. His abrupt departure had left her no choice but to address the miffed congress, "He'll send us provision, you'll see." This was makeshift verse that pelted Leong Shee in the heart.

For she heard nothing from the geezer, and instead, she heard bawling from her four-month-old San Tong, and more wails of hunger from her two-year-old San You.

Years passed without word from Jue Joe. And mind you, December through January was pirate season in Sum Gong Village. When the night crept close, Leong Shee hurried her two sons into the darkness of rice fields and hid each son inside a stack of rice straw for the night. Here, the boys would sleep, each inside their own stack of rice straw. At dawn Leong Shee reappeared to fetch her sons and bring them home. The alternative to her nightly ritual was unthinkable, for pirates kidnapped boys in Sum Gong Village and held them for ransom, especially if they were sons of "Gold Mountain" men.

"I didn't cry when my mother left me in that stack of rice straw," recounted my father San Tong Jue. He continued, "Each night during pirate season it was a different stack of straw that she would hide me in. Mother did the same for my older brother, too."

"How old were you?" I asked my father, foisting my ears forward at our dining table; this table was our family's collection point that drew my siblings to the congress as well. In our new home that Father had built in 1945 on the Jue Joe Ranch, in Van Nuys, California, dinner was a time in which vivid stories of Father's youth in Sum Gong Village cranked alive. He worked razor-sharp memories down our souls: Chinese teachings, ancient proverbs, they reared from a hidden corner of his interior; village customs, timeless traditions, they swooped us into the authenticity of a faraway world. It booted us onto a mysterious landscape colored by the sweep of dreams.

"I was about four or five-years old," responded Father. "In Winter, nights were so cold in our home that you didn't want to get out of bed; houses in Sum Gong had no heating system. But inside a stack of rice straw, I can say, your body is warmed by that cocoon. I did not feel alone or afraid. A blanket of stars lit the fields, and I was soothed by smells of rice straw and the soil soft as cotton surrounding my nest. I could breathe well by arranging a tiny opening to welcome the night's fresh air. So, on those winter haunts during pirate season I slept sound until my mother fetched me at daybreak. Then, I walked with her to retrieve my brother San You in another stack of straw, and the three of us padded home to have a bowl of rice porridge for breakfast. I can still recall how good that bowl of hot jook tasted!

"The rhythm of village life is simple and harmonious with nature," continued Father. "This is because all those whom you trust are contained within the walls of a village. It is a small, real world that you can cover within a day's walk. For your safety does not exist outside those walls; there is no police or government authority that regulates your life or protects you from harm. Only the elders in your clan council in a village looks after you."

After dinner, Father pushed aside his dinner plate and leaned forward to convey something curious. A faraway look took his countenance, and I heard his voice sketch a thought into shape for us.

"At night each household in Sum Gong Village had to donate a son for one week to stand guard atop a wall that surrounds our Village. Households worked in groups of ten armed guards that rotated each week atop that wall. On the hour I would hear a guard sound a gong to let you know that all was clear. But there were nights in which I would hear an explosion of gunfire exchanged between guards and pirates. Then just as suddenly the night fell silent.

"Although I was too young to participate, I grew curious. It was my cousin Ah Fook's turn to stand watch on that wall. So, I sneaked up the wall to join Ah Fook. He and I began to talk of little things, and I put my face up to the sky and saw tin lights so bright and close that I felt I could pluck them into a basket. In that instant Ah Fook caught a movement from the corner of his eye. There was no time to think. I saw Ah Fook hit the trigger of his rifle.

"Trembling, I heard sobbing and it emitted from me. Ah Fook and I saw that a fellow guardsman took that bullet by mistake. In Sum Gong Village you aged by a split-second of life's decisions and Cousin Ah Fook who was sixteen years of age, now squirreled between his brows the distress of an eighty-year-old."

Satisfied from a full meal, Father leaned back from the dining table. He opened wide his craw and uncorked to my siblings and me, "Now I bring up this point to show you that...." (Blah blah blah.) He lectured to our growing minds for the greater part of our youthful years. For dinner time was also lesson time.

I tell you that Father was a good storyteller, but he could bring up our shortcomings in the same sentence too. And these were astronomical according to Father: He had given us too much in life. We didn't understand what life was like back in the old country. We weren't alert and now we're running haywire. So, it was his duty to teach us to strive for success intelligently, and to apply critical thinking in our daily lives. But most important, Father stressed to my siblings and me the following:

We must never forget our duty to family because this is where our strength gleans from. Make no mistake about it. In Chinese thought: the family, and not the individual, is the smallest unit in society. So, for centuries the strength of this value is how Chinese civilization has been so resilient.

"Children are like weeds growing wild," wheeled Father's vote. "You must bend each weed with care and shape it as it grows. And one day, you will step back to admire a graceful bonsai plant."

I heard Father take us back to his yesteryear.

"Inside my cocoon of rice straw, I would listen for my mother's footsteps in the morning. She moved with uneven shuffles because her feet had been bound by an auntie when she was a little girl. This auntie was well-meaning when she bound my mother's feet with strips of white cloth. The auntie obeyed local custom for girls of my mother's age. But the pain my mother felt in her new bindings grew unbearable for her. She screamed so much and wept nonstop that this auntie finally ripped the squeezers off her."

Dawn fanned across a patchwork of cones in an open field. Overnight, those gleaming stacks of rice straw stood firm but one, one splayed by a boy who rose to rub his eyes. San Tong accepted the pungent air that rushed his lungs. The mix of animal smells and morning dew, the sound of bees, varmints, and human what-nots on the stir brought to San Tong a new day's start. This was the rhythm of village life throughout the Pearl River delta of Guangdong Province. And in the middle of this simplicity stood Sum Gong Village, a throwback to an ancient Song Dynasty's secret lore.

San Tong cleared straw from his loose, hand-spun trousers. A rip at one knee bared his skin and you could see Leong Shee's attempt to close that gap, but the worn muslin cloth had lost its hold long ago. I remind you that once a year, when harvest season was over, Leong Shee would spin her thread and sew by hand one new top-and-trouser for each of her two sons: San You and San Tong. And on New Year's Day the boys would don their new dressings, which would have to last them throughout the year until the next New Year's Day. Life was frugal and practical; nothing was ever waisted.

This monotonous daily repairing consumed the folks of Sum Gong Village. In less than an hour their clatter of laughter, gossip, spanking of earth, and pulling up weeds will bend through fields to shatter an early morning's silence.

At a distant edge of one field a veil of cooking smoke corkscrewed up one compound of homes. It comprised Jue Joe's grey-brick dwellings that he had built in 1903. His compound stood out because the grey fortress was not typical of other homes forged in Sum Gong Village, which were earthen huts parked so closely together that you could shove your hand out a window and brain your neighbor's meddling.

Jue Joe's brick fortress backed up against Snake Mountain to throw at you its Old West countenance. His interconnected rectangular homes were arranged to join the lives of his large extended family: the main house of Jue Joe's compound was a two-story affair. It was surrounded by smaller one-story sanctums, each home given to a brother and his family to sleep at night. This is because the main two-story house, which was occupied by Jue Joe as the patriarch of his extended family, was where communal activities took place daily among all members of his extended family. The main house saw adults cook and eat together; it saw little cousins study and play together. And when bandits breached Sum Gong Village's wall, when the nogooders brained Hangmei District's residents, the main house saw all Jue Joe's family shelter in its belly. For Jue Joe made sure that his two-story abode sported gun holes beneath its eaves, and next to those peek-a-boos, he attached planks of bamboo that you could lay on to shoot from.

Four kitchens. Each scullery claimed a corner of Jue Joe's main house that faced southwest: two in front warmed by the day's strong sunlight, and two in the rear primed to welcome generations to come. The grey-brick fortress was also a blend of two worlds. Jue Joe's family slept on western mattresses filled with down feathers, and not on raised wooden platforms that locals called a "kang." Each bed was crafted in the Old West style. Meaning that each bedframe sprang up bedposts carved in simple design.

So there, there in Sum Gong Village in the residential district of Hangmei rose the power of one man's hour: a dreamhouse colored in battleship grey. The old brick compound still stands today as it had in 1903 to house the lifestyles of four families: Jue Nui who was the oldest of Jue Joe's siblings and who emigrated to Monterey, California; Jue Joe who was brother #2 who built the compound and lived in its main house as I said earlier; Jue Shee who was brother #3 who later emigrated to Los Angeles, California; and Jue Yau who was the youngest brother #4 who never left the compound at all.

I should add at this point that in the absence of word from Jue Joe, who had sailed to California for a second time to rebuild his fortune, Leong Shee believed that he had perished in San Francisco's 1906 Earthquake. As a result, she morphed into a widow struggling to flounce her wits. One day her five older brothers arrived from Ma Choong Village to teach her how to farm, how to give lip at an open bazaar, and how to manage monsoon rivalries in a man's business world. Soon, Sum Gong's fierce sun caught sight of a self-reliant widow, and her two sons looked on the upswing of being well-fed. Leong Shee saw to it that Jue Joe's extended family was cared for too.

A fishpond foists on you more than a scrap of beauty. Its magical world molds for you something very Chinese. You may find in it a swarm of carp, some eels, or a family of turtles mixed in. Needing no invite, there's a handful of frogs prancing round lily pads too. Leong Shee's fishpond in front of Jue Joe's compound was twelve-feet deep and twenty-feet wide. Two bamboo buckets loitered at its lip. Nearby, a shoulder pole lingered on the ground; it would rest on your shoulder to balance the buckets evenly when filled.

Plunging his bucket into the pond and bringing it upright, San Tong captured live carp quivering from Leong Shee's hand-dug hole. He steadied the pole across his shoulders. There is a way to gallop with laden buckets without tiring yourself, and San Tong learned it, learned to trot at a steady gait, allowing his pole to bounce in rhythm, then he increased his stride and speed without breaking his momentum.

And of Jue Joe's flushing toilet? It was forever imbedded in San Tong's interior. Jue Joe had installed a high tank pull chain toilet on the second-floor balcony of his main house. And this Western toilet was attached to a brick wall by an open window of San Tong's bedroom. The toilet served a strategic stratagem: It was not roomed downstairs because adult visitors to Jue Joe's home knew nothing of how a flushing toilet worked. This was because folks were familiar with a hole in the ground and knew that spreading wood ash over that hole tamped unpleasant odors quite efficiently. Instead, Western technology was placed purposefully upstairs by Jue Joe because a high tank toilet was a status symbol for his sons to appreciate. San You and San Tong would be reminded that their father had graced the exotic land of Gum Saan. It would infuse excitement, education for his sons to ruminate. And so, this far-away import would lift the family's prestige degrees higher than others who were not as fortunate.

But I tell you that a flushing toilet was nightmare for two boys in a backwater hamlet. Plumbing had not yet been introduced to Sum Gong Village. So, daily San You and San Tong fetched buckets of water from a river located a morning's walk away. And upon arriving home, they had to climb up steep stairs to the second floor without spilling their buckets. Reaching the bamboo hopper that Jue Joe had installed, it was hard for the boys to lift their heavy buckets over the tank's wicker top to keep that darn thing filled. Of course, there was a water well located on the north side of the main house, but when you peered down its depth—it flashed you an echo of your voice. The well fell dry weeks after Jue Joe had skirted for Los Angeles.

Nevertheless, this Western miracle caught attention. There was a cut-out seat placed on top of a bucket that had a hole drilled through its bottom, and a tube attached to that small opening meandered down two stories. When you tugged a French chain on Jue Joe's hopper you heard a great flood rush from the high tank's wicker basket, and by gravitation, it fertilized Leong Shee's vegetables in her outside garden.

Truth be told, Jack, latrines hold stories. In the case of Jue Joe's high tank pull chain toilet, its wicker basket warped during Sum Gong's extreme winters and humid summers, and as a result, it fell to whimper and then to zero use.

Yesterday, Leong Shee struck a deal with her two granny neighbors. Together they purchased a piggy. They would feed and raise this piggy to maturity. And when the porker morphed into a blimp, well, they would hawk that hog at market and split the proceeds. This was their gambit.

Their hog, of course, promoted pluck. Since it was allowed to run free, that is what it did. The pig knew which day and which neighbor to visit for its meal. It knew what time to appear at that neighbor's doorstep and how much of a portion it was entitled to consume. And if the pig did not receive its rightful portion, you heard the loudest squealing for redress against such impudence.

One day the prized pig vanished. To Leong Shee's horror she saw a corkscrew tail protruding from her fishpond. A monsoon had swallowed Sum Gong Village and in that instant the pig slipped from the pond's edge into oblivion. When the turns of weather cleared its rudder, two grannies in Leong Shee's trio shot about ballistic. This was their livelihood lost, wagged their tongues at Leong Shee. This happened on YOUR WATCH, pumped a truth among the biddies, blah, blah, blah.

To purchase their peace, Leong Shee forked over ten catties of rice, twenty tamales of sticky rice with side-bits swaddled in banana leaves, two bags of tangerine peels, and two earthen jars filled with dried dates. This village-style surrender proved acceptable to the grannies, and it moved forward the rhythm of rural life for all parties once again.

Now I pause a moment on the word "survival." A big canal that divides Sum Gong Village in half runs quite urgent. It is wide enough to be mistaken for a small river. After a monsoon's torrid tantrum, well, the canal's character becomes every youngster's muddy lap pool. Or if you've misread its mood swings, it speeds you downstream to the next village without compunction or into Neptune's coffee-colored lair. I kid you not.

But this is how children learn survival: coursing round Sum Gong's canals and rivers. The morning turned vivid and hot the day that six-year-old San You and four-year-old San Tong arrived at the big canal. Today was San Tong's notable day. He would take the canal for the first time, and his brother San You would prompt him through it. And so, San You parked San Tong at a clump of shade where waters below them appeared to cast a calm smile.

San Tong felt the tendrils of a thousand-year-old mangrove tree grasp his hand and lead the rest of him down a steep bank into briny waters. Old, thick limbs that curled round his tiny paw pushed its whiffs of slime up his nostrils, it sallied forth centuries of Sum Gong's secret mire sailing down his arm. Entwined in knots and gnarls, San Tong's lower half began to tread the canal's dark history, practicing his scissor kicks and figure eights while clinging to old-man mangrove.

Then a force broke free. For a monsoon's headwind roiled its swagger to rip away the character of the canal's peace. Hands of the mangrove tree untethered San Tong.

In that instant trouble swallowed him. San Tong hadn't learned to tread a rapid. Swift swirls dragged his cartoon-sized eyes downstream, nose bobbing, his remaining torso enfolded in the vortex of a dark antiquity. San Tong heard the ground above him shriek with a familiar voice. He felt the vibration of his brother San You's footsteps pounding after him. Like old-man mangrove, San You's tendrils reached for San Tong and dragged him up and onto grass.

"That was close," admitted San You. He clouted San Tong's chest to make him chug up briny water. Then San You stripped away his little brother's cottons to wring the clothes of water. He spread soggy top and trouser across that whiskery carpet for the burning sun to quench its thirst.

"Don't you tell Ma what happened!" implored San You. He expelled more thought, "She'll whomp us!" For good measure, San You stalled their journey home. They laid on grass for hours; its sweet smell lifted their dreams far from the moment. In time the sun satisfied itself of thirst and drew low across the horizon. And as light fired one last glow, San You signalled his little brother to get dressed. Days pushed forward and there he was: San Tong returned to the canal alone and taught himself how to swim.

Jue Joe's main house was big country: many voices bent through the vastness of its chambers; cooking smoke from four kitchens corkscrewed daily up through eves. There were two kitchens in the front corners of his house and two in the back corners, as I have said, which were placed according to the traditional four corners of cosmic earth.

Leong Shee's front kitchen had a window that fixed her eye on four lichee trees outside, pregnant with fruit. The trees were planted by Jue Joe when he built the compound in 1903 for his three brothers and himself. His compound was designed for an extended family in which each brother and his family had a small house for their privacy, but all members congregated at Jue Joe's main house for daily cooking, dining, social activities, and for doing communal chores. This was in accordance with Chinese custom.

Upstairs in Jue Joe's main house each of the four bedrooms connected to a central, open landing in which there was a long table and benches for all the little cousins to do their schoolwork together. On that upper floor, two bedrooms on each side of the second floor shared a sitting room between themselves as well. And downstairs, well, that was Jue Joe's master bedroom that he shared with his wife Leong Shee. It was important that their master bedroom and kitchen be in the "southwest corner" of their home. This is because *feng shui* identifies the southwest site as an "earth corner" that sets in motion a harmonious environment inside a home: the position reveals feminine attributes such as kitchen, nurturing, and an ability to deliver abundance.

I tell you that *feng shui* dominates the construction of a Chinese home and the placement of objects around the home because, when properly fused together, the synergy produces harmonious relationships that reinforce *unity*. And unity, mind you, is a central value held deep within the interior of Chinese thinking; the concept has stood the test of time down through the ages.

However, one thing messed up *feng shui*. "A toilet from the West!" pumped the craw of a local. "What!? He has no hole in the ground?" flicked a biddy in response. Soon ditty flew in multiples round Sum Gong Village. For countrymen returning home from Gum Saan (Gold Mountain) who could afford such a status symbol, well, they were held in high esteem by the locals. This is because foreign symbols projected innovative gambit. It was an armchair expedition away from a monotonous routine of weeding and repairing in the life of a villager.

To be sure, Jue Joe's sons would show their cousins and friends in the same generation how to navigate such a Western complexity; and hopefully, future technologies would open for the YOU WHO ARE YET TO BE BORN. Chinese think in the long-term.

For the adults, however, Jue Joe made sure that his main house reflected two cultures in this way: the outside doors were constructed in accordance with local custom; meaning that they had iron rings for chain and padlock. But inside doors were made in the Western style: they had doorknobs to turn for opening and closing the doors. Nevertheless, Leong Shee in her downstairs kitchen fired up her stove by pumping a bellow below her brick range. The rice straw that she used for firewood burned well and long.

Approaching the front gate of Jue Joe's main house—you will find it locked. Always, it is locked. The *feng shui* (wind and water) went squirrelly. It was rumored by neighbors that, when the house was built, the energy had scattered. This is because in getting plastered on rice wine at the start, a local builder hired by Jue Joe had forgotten *feng shui* in the construction. At once folks feared the worst.

"She is going to kill us all!" exclaimed Leong Shee's neighbors among themselves.

"Her front door opens south when it should open east or west if she respects heaven's cosmic order. Now, bad things will come to us all," worked more craws. "Evil spirits can run straight lines, as in Jue Joe's north to south doors. But they cannot run a broken line, as in doors running east and west. This breaks the evil spirits' access."

"That's why gardens have zigzag pathways," creamed a biddy at Leong Shee. "That's why windows are shaped octagonal, have you forgotten?"

"If you open that south door—good things leave!" wagged the oldest of an old-timer. "And YOU give nogooders food, too, I seen it! They are P-I-R-A-T-E-S! Need I spell out more? No *feng shui* means no good luck for us all," punted the proud granny.

How folks complained. In no time it grew to a wag throughout Sum Gong Village.

To make amends, Leong Shee tied strings of firecrackers above the front door of Jue Joe's house; fortuitous words slid down the front door's posts. Then she hung symbols of good fortune written on red paper above that entrance: the Five Happiness. And finally, she coughed up five silver coins for a geomancer to reposition Jue Joe's two side doors to run more properly the east-west axis. And these doors brought her luck.

The heavens threw a smile on Leong Shee and grew her confidence. In time she added thirty-three new acres to Jue Joe's land. Trundling pushcarts and flatbeds swollen with content to an open bazaar, which was located on the other side of the big canal, Leong Shee took the commercial district of Dai Jan by storm. Throngs gathered with eagerness as Leong Shee squat herself on gravel and exposed her baskets of wrinkled cabbage, goose eggs, string beans, sweet potatoes, sugar cane, and rice that glistened in the humidity of the noonday's sun.

You heard Leong Shee nod and laugh and engage folks in conversation as they strolled by. Her gentle manner and kind words pulled people to her. And she spread her knowledge of farming techniques to all who would listen; she enjoyed that moment.

But at home beneath the shade of four lichee trees Leong Shee's demeanor grew pensive. She longed for companionship of the real kind, but these four trees alone remained her faithfuls. And as the seasons swept bare the leaves on her lychee trees and turned their limbs brittle, Leong Shee saw her arms and flesh foretell of the same hollows. Mind you, she was not yet thirty years of age.

A man like Jue Joe defines your destiny, drummed a corner of Leong Shee's interior, you can never escape your ghosts.

Slowly, Leong Shee found strength as she worked the whir of her spinning wheel. Under the four lichee trees she sat and spun fibers of coarse cotton as she listened to the wheel's squeaks and then adjusted the feed of the yarn. She slapped and rolled each fiber against her thigh, and when she had enough balls of yarn, she ran a needle through her hair to oil its tip. Once a year Leong Shee sewed by hand one new top and trouser for each of her two sons. The coarse muslin cloth was made to be thick—strong enough to withstand a year's wear for her two sons. This is because the new field clothes would have to last her sons a whole year—until the next New Years Day. This was the way of village life in Sum Gong's parlance.

If a man stretched miles between the both of you, squirreled Leong Shee's interior round and round, if he deserted his family by sailing into infinity without having returned for his two sons, well, how can you begin to fill that void?

She was living the answer.

CHAPTER 3 - A STRANGER'S VISIT

A man's moody eyes were lost in thought as he bent through winter to reach a train station. The snow barrelled round his boots and a powerful gale whipped his long hair into streaks. His brother must be back in Los Angeles, circled memories within this man's interior, he's there and not in Sum Gong Village.

The man paused before his train. He had left his tedious job at the Ford Motor Assembly plant in Harbin, Manchuria, as World War I shook awake the planet in 1914. So, in that whirling blizzard the man held tightly the hand of his fourteen-year-old son whose mother had recently died. She was the man's Manchurian wife who—in the maelstrom of war's madness—had succumbed to a stray bullet unleashed in the chaos of combat. And now, now the man's focus was safety for his son and for himself.

Jue Shee wanted to be a mining engineer. He had never gotten the degree in America, but he knew there were so many treasures hidden in the soil of Sum Gong

Village: platinum, iron, zinc, and so forth. He and his son would have to trek southward—a long way—to make good his desire to be a mining engineer. For he had only to dig those big dreams up in Sum Gong Village, revved Jue Shee's interior engine.

Hiking down the arc of a timeless China, Jue Shee's mind toggles between two dialects, two lifestyles that seem worlds apart, it all rests on the regions that a sojourner enters in the vastness of this Land. In this case the mind springs him into an old habit.

He read books. He knew how to mine. And the precious metals would fetch him high prices in a wartime market. This habit would sweep him round the upswings of life.

Yes, books. Books can set a mind free, believed Jue Shee. He remembers sitting in a classroom in the Christian Missionary School in Pasadena, California, trying to read English letters on pages of a book propped in front of him. His brother Jue Joe had paid for his emigration from China more than twenty years ago. The Chinese Exclusion Act of 1882 had prevented him from using his real name, so Jue Joe had arranged a paper name for his brother to circumnavigate the Law with authorities at Angel Island Immigration Station.

Jue Joe set his brother Jue Shee to work on his potato farm in the San Fernando Valley. But Jue Shee hated that work and dreamed of learning English and going to college and becoming a mining engineer. So, his brother let him take time off to attend a school with other Chinese adult students. He remembered enrolling in the school, and they had asked his name. He couldn't bring himself to use his false paper name, so he used his real name, "Jue Shee." He was a proud man. He was glad his teacher trained him to write English letters for his name. Yes, his real name.

As the train departs and his son falls asleep there are more memories. He remembers his two friends: Fong Foo Sec who was attending Pomona College and would ultimately go to UC Berkeley, and one of Fong Sec's friends Walter Ngon Fong who was attending Stanford. Fong Sec had told Jue See that after he studied and acquired fluency in English at the Christian Missionary School, he should apply for the college preparatory school at Pomona College, and afterwards, enroll in its college courses. When completed, he could transfer to UC Berkeley which is just what Fong Sec had done.

More books. Jue Shee remembers signing his name to his books in the college preparatory classes at Pomona College and sitting with teenagers half his age. At thirty-seven-years of age, Jue Shee remembers their sniggers, their whispers about the "old Chinaman" sitting amongst them.

He remembers the Orpheum Theater in Los Angeles, too.

"Can't you read?" said a five-foot doorman to Jue Shee and his two Chinese friends. In the lobby of the Orpheum Theater the squeak pointed to a sign posted in English, "No Chinese allowed." The doorman returned his fixed expression on the trio, "Well, read it!"

Ragtime tunes belted from behind a red velvet curtain. Al Jolson's new movie, which was Los Angeles' first "talkie," was premiering. Jue Shee wore a new suit for the special occasion. A silk tie roped shut the neck of his starched shirt; a bright handkerchief popped from his breast pocket too. Now, the three young men pretended they did not understand the English words written on the sign in the Orpheum Theater's lobby.

Wherein the five-foot doorman screamed, "You Chinks get outta here!" He worked Jue Shee and his friends toward a door that led to a side alley, but the three men pushed themselves past the doorman. They parted the lobby's red velvet drapes and entered the warm glow of the Theater's womb. Rhinestones sparkling on women's coiffures bobbed in confusion. A woman screamed, "Go back where you…." White men rose from their folding chairs. With quickness the melee exploded: chairs flew, the projector quit, whistles blew, and you saw police wielding night sticks round the tattered womb.

Posting bail at the city jail, Jue Shee went to work with his plan. He was now an educated man: he filed a lawsuit against the Orpheum Theater for discrimination. Yes that. Jue Shee won this battle, too, and the Orpheum Theater was forced to open its doors to all paying customers. But in the scheme of things, it was only a small victory.

Jue Shee knew in his heart that, as a man in his mid-thirties, he was not cut out to do four years of college-prep at Pomona, then four more years at UC Berkeley to graduate, and finally, climb higher for an advanced degree in mining engineering. He had also heard from friends that Chinese with mining degrees could not find work in America. Doors were closed to Chinese, and he hated taking classes with those snickering white teenagers!

Yes, he had sold off Jue Joe's potato farm, had taken the cash and run to Paris, France, to experience the high life. Then he had gone back to China and settled in

Harbin to be far away from his aggrieved older brother. Now, Jue Shee would return to Sum Gong and tell all who would listen that he was a famous mining engineer from "Gold Mountain" who would soon find riches in the soil for all in Sum Gong Village.

There they were. The stranger and his son sliding into view at Leong Shee's side door. He raised the issue of her filial duty. "I'm no imposter! I am YOUR husband's brother," he emphasized. Claiming his rightful honor, Jue Shee defended his stake in the Jue family's estate. Meaning one for all and all for one in the Chinese tradition. It was the wondrous, painful, loving, and practical root-power of the meaning of family duty in the Chinese equation. At once Leong Shee understood that she had no alternative but to accept Jue Shee's stratagem and downgrade her rank in Jue Joe's clan.

She pushed her tiny torso forward to address Jue Shee. And with her lips pursed, asked how—on the other side of time—had Jue Joe died.

"Jue Joe? Sister, he's in Los Angeles."

Cold dead silence filled Leong Shee's interior. Her mind leaned hard against his words as she stirred a wok in Jue Joe's kitchen. A thought tread round and round: nine years have passed and not a word from him. Why that old geezer--

"He's angry and after me," continued Jue Shee. "My mother's nephew, Lee Bing, wrote to warn me. I'm a dead man, he says. No, Jue Joe didn't perish in the Earthquake of 1906, in San Francisco. Together we farmed potatoes in the Southland, did you know that? Jue Joe would hitch four horses to his buck wagon—fill it to the brim with potato crates—and he would drive that wagon three hours from the San Fernando Valley and over the Cahuenga Pass to the Produce Exchange in central Los Angeles. Three hours each way! One day he said to Lee Bing and me, 'I'm gonna get me a wife.' Lee Bing and I roared with laughter. I said, 'Sure, sure, you so old she gotta get your coffin the day you get hitched.' Jue Joe replies, 'I'm serious, kid, I'm gonna marry in the old country.' And you know what? He turned his business right over to me. All I had to do was to send him some of the cash every month." Jue Shee threw an eye at Leong Shee to see what she thought of all this; what she tossed back to him was unequivocal stupefaction.

"When my brother married you," continued Jue Shee, "I figured he wouldn't be back to Los Angeles. So, I sold everything! What did I want with potatoes? I'm a mining engineer. I bought high-class tools and a one-way passage to Manchuria because the newspapers had told of a big gold strike near Harbin, with lots of guys getting rich who knew just how to dig it up." Jue Shee continued with the half-truths of his life.

"One day I came out of my tent and soldiers with fur hats and chin straps marched past me. The guy standing next to me whispered, 'They are Russians.' Later that afternoon I caught old Japanese ladies hidden in scarves and boots ripping Russian signposts for firewood. I might have stayed in Harbin and made a killing, but the Russo-Japanese war was on, and so, I got out of there as quickly as possible with my son to come home." Jue Shee knew how to shape a story with a ring of truth.

Leong Shee was not really listening, however. She was worried about the intrusion on her ordered world by this strange man. For Jue Shee took title to Jue Joe's compound in free simple, so to speak. And Leong Shee's eyes grew big as saucers at his impudence.

Jue Shee's gift to Leong Shee's corner of the world? A library. Using Leong Shee's savings he built a library attached to Jue Joe's main house. The two-story library weighted your mind with Western philosophy, the holy scriptures, rumblings of odd verse, and all the angles of science. But no one in Sum Gong Village could read; not English, and barely Chinese.

Nevertheless, Sum Gong's menfolk fell nightly into the crevice of Jue Shee's library. Leafing through a thick volume, the menfolk perused a picture of human anatomy—the lower half—and nodded knowingly and flashed high confidence. Leong Shee looked away in disgust. I tell you that by midnight the menfolk were drunk as skunks, and Leong Shee had to scrub their puke off the brick floor.

"It went on for my mother night after night," said Father one evening in our San Fernando Valley home. In the healthy days of life on the Jue Joe Ranch in Van Nuys, California, he always ended supper with the celebration of a story. It was lunar New Year and he'd washed his feet and donned a red flannel shirt, for the color red is auspicious in Chinese culture. Father told us, "Pretty soon you could shove your fingers down Ma's coin jar and mingle with air. One day Uncle Jue Shee unveiled a surprise on our balcony, too. Reading an English manual, he'd crafted his own machine gun. He was polishing that piece when it blew off, slicing our rooster in half in the garden below. My mother was so angry, but she had to cap her feelings in Uncle's presence of course."

Father paused to light his Lucky Strike cigarette. He blew clouds up the air that cancelled his face from my view, but then I heard him speak again. "Months flew by, and I found Ma and Uncle on the balcony squaring off. From the yard below I saw Uncle point his gun at Ma on the balcony, and he shouted, 'One shot—just one!—and you're history.' My mother began to sob uncontrollably."

"I remember the day Ma couldn't take it anymore. She began to throw Jue Shee's books out the window of his library." This is because Ma saw her sweet potatoes in the garden wither; her stalks of sugarcane splayed. She saw her carp in Jue Joe's fishpond float to the surface sideways; all dead. This was due to the rat-tat-tat of Jue Shee's mining drill. His machine kneaded the soil round our house, and nothing grew anymore; certainly, not peace of mind. Jue Shee's lust for platinum, zinc, and ore had whittled away my mother's bountiful earth.

"When Uncle realized what Ma had done with his books—he made her life so miserable," ran Father's turbine. "He sprang for his machine gun and aimed it straight between her eyes. I heard Uncle rip the air, 'I'm gonna kill you!' Then Uncle swerved that piece of metal down at me in the front yard! Clods of dirt kicked round my feet as slugs cracked the air. I ran and jumped into our fishpond as fast as I could. When I surfaced, I saw Ma's face white as flour. She was in the yard, patting blindly for all the books she'd vanquished to eternity. Just as quickly, she raced upstairs to the library and reinstated the works on shelves in Uncle's, well, hall of foreign learning."

A letter arrived. Leong Shee could not read it. She could not interpret Chinese characters well because girls were not given formal schooling in the old days; formal schooling was reserved for boys in Sum Gong Village. Now, Leong Shee wondered if the letter was from Jue Joe. Intrigued, she walked to a shop in Dai Jan District, across the big canal. The old man who sold wares to Leong Shee and who now banked her coins inside his safe could also read foreign mail. "It's from a letter writer in Los Angeles…about a Jue Joe," he told her. "Good news!" exclaimed the man. He drilled on, "'I'm well,' it says, 'I send you this.'" The old man in the general store flashed a banknote at Leong Shee. Pouring over the yellowed letter with his thick spectacles, which were pinched across the bridge of his nose, he asked her, "Do you want me to write to him?"

Leong Shee nodded in the affirmative. Studying a watermark brought to life by an oil lamp's flickers, Leong Shee was fascinated by the banknote's exotic character.

The old man lifted his Chinese brush to write. "Five coins, o.k.?" postured his voice.

"What!?" jumped Leong Shee's windpipe. "Too much! Short note is all I want." Their fingers threw themselves into shadow-play. They settled on two silver coins.

Down an inkwell plunged the old man's brush, "I will give you two columns for THREE silver coins," upped his ante.

In the shadow of the oil lamp, two silhouettes played hammer- and-scissors until the old man acquiesced and added a third column at no extra charge. Mark my words, Leong Shee was a seasoned marketeer.

The man wrote as Leong Shee spoke her words. From Leong Shee to Jue Joe: "You don't know my misery—your brother's going to blow us up! Do something! Signed-X."

Jue Joe sat in his one-room cabin with a dirt floor. A roar from his potbelly stove pitched him warmth on a winter's night in the San Fernando Valley. He sat by that black-iron belly that snapped red-ember glows across his corded face. For Leong Shee's letter rocked about in his hand. Although he could not read, he had had a letter writer in Los Angeles' Chinatown voice aloud the content of her mouthpiece to him. And now, now Jue Joe dropped his wife's strife into flares of oblivion in that stove.

In Jue Joe's cabin you glimpsed his box-spring bed and the absence of bedsheets. There was a fruit crate that stood by his bedside, and on that crate, a kerosene lamp stretched a dim light across Jue Joe's face as he lay in bed. It lit up the mood of his interior: spare, dark with thought, and worn from time. There were farm tools and leather horse-harnesses tacked to walls of his cabin, too, and one saddle straddled a wine barrel.

In Jue Joe's depths, he dug up a vague vision of Leong Shee. But the years of separation gave up no more. Important to this old-timer were questions he posed in air: Are my sons well? Have they grown smart? My two sons San You and San Tong must bring honor to our family. My brother, Jue Shee, had gone his crazy way and I swear that my sons will do better.

And what of me? He threw idea against four walls of his clapboard cabin. I suppose it is time for me to be a family man again.

And so, there came for Leong Shee and her two sons in Sum Gong Village a list for them to memorize. It was ninety-pages long. Included were three First-Class tickets aboard the *SS Columbia* steamer bound for San Francisco, California, too. The following signature authenticated their permit: "Oliver, Attorney at Law."

"You got to have a lawyer," wrote Jue Joe in a final letter to Leong Shee. "It's the American way." So, Leong Shee folded these treasures into her cloth travel bag.

It was a soft August night on our Jue Joe Ranch, Jack. I heard crickets sing from Father's hibiscus bushes. I smelled scrub fresh as dew along our avenue. And I felt the pastel rhythms of my summer. As Father's lantern paused before our big barn's open door, I caught sight of Jue Joe's horse-harnesses hanging high on the Redwood walls of that barn. Then Father slid the squeaking barn door shut. Together we walked slowly to the front lawn, joining the family gathering under the vault of that moving, onyx sky. My family and I spread ourselves upon blankets and gazed up at stars twinkling back their quiet language, and this reminded Father to tell us something.

"It was a night like this," said Father, "our ship gliding silently over a calm ocean. At least, it felt this way in our First-Class cabin. Around 3:00 am, my brother San You whispered in our mother's ear that we should go to the deck. There, I watched my mother unfold Oliver's documents that San You had read to her. As the *SS Columbia* steamer carried the three of us across the dateline to our destination in San Francisco, I felt my mother's nervousness.

"She said to us, 'When we reach the Port of San Francisco your Father's going to say this and say that to the authorities. He must answer their tricky questions, and we'll have to match his story in every little detail. The authorities ask you lots and lots of questions full of details. Your Father wrote us, '…and remember exactly where the kerosene lamp sits in my house in Sum Gong Village, and where the hopper hangs too. Memorize how the sun turns through my kitchen's window and which of the four kitchens we use. Also, remember where the wok in the kitchen is placed…where my house is located, and where my brothers' homes are too. You have got to know the distance that my lichee trees are from my house, and how many trees there are, and who planted them. Don't forget to explain in which direction Sum Gong Village's main road runs….'

"Well, that was ninety pages to embed in our minds. But absorb those details we did. Afterwards, we stole to a lower deck at the Ship's rear where the early morning took its darkest character, and I remember shredding the Oliver evidence into waves churning us toward San Francisco, California."

"San Francisco," continued Father, "to me it was like coming into a wild adventure. I felt terror at the possibility of goofing an interrogation conducted by the U.S. Immigration authorities. For the authorities will separate you because of a stupid error you may make, separate you from your family and send you back to China by yourself. It happened to many families who made errors and gave wrong answers. And the pain of this horror lasts for generations, you know. A family's continuity once severed may never heal and that is a hard move felt in silence by so many."

On the *SS Columbia* that night so long ago, my father was just thirteen-years old. For him Jue Joe seemed a mythical vision, the father he didn't know but imagined that he knew. The voyage had taken a month, and the end was near as the Vessel brought his mother Leong Shee, his brother San You, and himself toward a tall and wondrous glass city.

Arriving at Angel Island's Immigration Station, San Francisco from a short distance across the bay looked like neat rows of colorful dollhouses, said my father San Tong. With borrowed binoculars he noted homes with high-pitched roofs, ornate woodwork on gables, and slender turrets; oh, they were quite pretty but so unlike Chinese villages. He was anxious to explore what this new world was about.

CHAPTER 4 – JUE JOE IN CALIFORNIA, ACT TWO

When I think of the San Fernando Valley, Jack, I remember its serenity like the low murmur of a song, sonorous. When the sun dropped low on the horizon, I'd hear a coyote's cry bend through the Valley; I'd hear the craw of crickets pierce the night with urgency, reminding me of the vastness of nature's tenor. Then I'd catch the brilliance of a moon rise to cast its care across a stretch of silent fields. The San Fernando Valley for me was made of old family farms, acres of farms as far as your eye could see. It was filled with plow horses tacking slowly down those fields, and chickens complaining, and cats scratching round, and wet laundry hung out in sunlight to dry. This was the Valley's natural rhythm, and it brought to all who ventured onto its soil—a wealth of spirit for the human character. This was so for Jue Joe.

The year of 1906 returned Jue Joe to the San Fernando Valley for his second act. Jue Shee had frittered away his fortune. At age fifty, Jue Joe felt goosed. The shame of a kid brother's treason twisted down his spine, frisked his ulcer, flew up to flood his eyes. The family in China must never know the details of Jue Shee's dishonor. This is what Jue Joe reminded himself.

My little brother up and left, left us all to fend for ourselves, rang gongs in Jue Joe's interior. And there's nothing to speak of the years that I have toiled in California to keep our family fed: first as a migrant in the vineyards of Napa, then as a railroad worker earning peanuts on the San Luis Obispo line, and finally, tilling the good earth and building a business in a remote, northwest valley of Los Angeles. How Jue Joe's engine revved with uncontrollable feeling.

Then it happened. Jue Joe had to reconstruct his game just as he'd learned to do in his first act in America. He found himself plowing the San Fernando Valley's lore once more, giving life to potato spuds that had been his fortune in his first act. It was hard work for an old man, but Jue Joe knew the Valley's heartbeat. He knew how to make things grow on its fertile soil.

However, I backtrack to tell you the following: In 1906, when Jue Joe arrived in Los Angeles again, he had to work as a houseboy. Yes, this again. He was a fifty-year-old China Boy taking orders and serving a Lo-Fan husband and his wife in their splendid home that was built for entertaining. Jue Joe served them with a smile, always with that fixed smile. For he took any job whether humble or difficult to survive and provide for his family. This was the measure of the man. He was focused on production, and in time, he saved enough cash to lease some land and grow potato spuds in the San Fernando Valley once more. Old Joe felt lucky to obtain the land because Chinese-born farmers were subject to discriminatory Exclusion Laws aimed at them in the agricultural industry; but Jue Joe had the trust of powerful friends in the white community who helped him secure the coveted farmland in the Valley. So, he bid farewell to his Lo-Fan master and mistress.

However I will now go back even further and tell you the tale of Joe's first act in California. Jue Joe was born in 1856. Jue Joe remembers his early years well. His first hint of life was being born in a chicken coop. He heard the hens and one cock sound off against his intrusion. And as he grew older, he discovered that his parents were dirt poor farmers in Sum Gong Village. So, at eighteen-years of age, which was his Chinese age (you add one year for time in the womb as I have told you before), young Jue Joe vowed that his family would never experience such poverty again. On this pledge he left for Hong Kong hoping to find passage to "Gum Saan," which means "Gold Mountain" in Anglo-translation, as I've said to you earlier. Make no mistake. This teenager had a knack for finding work. Jue Joe signed on as a cabin boy for First-Class passengers on the *SS Japan.* It was an all wooden, sidewheel steamer bound for San Francisco that was commissioned by President Abraham Lincoln just before his assassination.

That day, standing beside the *SS Japan,* widow Lee Shee gave her son Jue Joe sixteen pounds of rice—all that she could afford—to defer the costs of buying food onboard the Ship during its long Pacific sailing.

In 1874 Jue Joe arrived in San Francisco. He had only one-quarter pound of rice left after more than a month's journey. He hoped that the Chinese Six Companies in San

Francisco's Chinatown could change his fate. The elders of this Benevolent Association referred him to a labor boss who supplied Chinese workers for Napa Valley's vineyards. Jue Joe worked first in Marysville, and then in St. Helena, harvesting grapes, stomping grapes, churning vats of grapes, dreaming grapes until he fell asleep in the wee hours.

And there, there in St. Helena Jue Joe spent long days stooping and picking you-know-what in a vineyard. As he padded slowly back to Chinatown one day—his back pounding with pain—he felt the paws of a Lo-Fan nogooder brain him. No, no, it was a group of bullies who jumped him.

"Hey, Chink, you go back where you came from. We don't want you here!" shouted one among the white bullies. Then the congress pummelled Jue Joe to the ground. And as proof of such impudence, Jue Joe sported a gash over his right eyebrow and a broken little finger from this flail that would last him a lifetime.

From that day forward, he slept with a cleaver pushed under his pillow and wagged round a loaded Colt .44 as a sidearm. But the day that good citizens of St. Helena marched into Chinatown and demanded that *all* Chinese leave or they would burn the place down—lynch a Chink who dared stay—well, on that lather, Jue Joe understood it was time to hightail for other pastures.

Nine Chinese and Jue Joe left St. Helena and found themselves at a railroad yard in Oakland, California. Here, boss men from the Southern Pacific were looking for men cheap as they could get to lay the rails southward along the coast—all the way down to Los Angeles.

"Hell, you got no finer busters than these Chinamen!" exclaimed a Hong Kong man who contracted Chinese laborers to the railroad bosses. The Hong Konger straddled a railroad iron that lay rusting in the yard. Mud peeled off his calf-high boots as he kicked the iron for emphasis. He pulled a billed cap low on his forehead and pitched to railroad bosses, "Look no further my good men—I have your answer right here." He hustled flesh before the railroad barons like a barker at a roadside cathouse. "You got this machine for a buck a day," wagged his larynx, he pushed Jue Joe by the collar to a railroad boss.

Chinese surrendered to such a mood. They needed work. They forked one-fourth of their buck-a-day earnings to the Hong Konger who ran his lucrative credit-ticket operation in Oakland's Chinatown. On the other side of the world, this Hong Konger had a partner in China who convinced poor locals to exchange their skills for the cost of their passage to America.

So, young Jue Joe took a section gang's job busting for the Southern Pacific. But he was not told about the harsh terrain that awaited him. No one dared question the authorities about conditions on the job—or the job went to someone else. So, Jue Joe began to lay tracks from San Luis Obispo southward to Santa Barbara, where a connecting line that ran from Los Angeles was scheduled to meet them at Santa Barbara.

There was sadness in Jue Joe's eyes. He learned the fate of his older brother Jue Nui in Alaska. From Sum Gong Village, Jue Nui had crossed the big ocean on cash that his younger brother had earned picking grapes in Marysville and St Helena. This included cash that Jue Joe had been loaned from St. Helena's Chinatown "Wui." The Wui was an association of Chinese merchants who pooled together cash to loan to a member who offered the highest bid on his payback interest. Jue Joe coughed up the highest bid based on his calculated earnings from the Southern Pacific Railroad.

Jue Nui's first job was for a large Chinese canning company in Monterey, California. From there Jue Nui had signed on to work on an oil platform in Alaska. But the ship that carried Jue Nui and other Chinese workers to Alaska hit a terrible storm. "Worse storm in twenty years," it was said. The ship sunk with all passengers and crew lost at sea in the Bay of Alaska.

Nineteenth-century news relayed like a snail. Four months after Jue Nui's sudden drowning, Jue Joe received the big shock. Months later in the year, Jue Joe received another shock. It was a letter from his mother Lee Shee in Sum Gong Village.

"It's your fault I lost my boy," banged her craw. Lee Shee continued her mourning, "Your news about Gum Saan made him want to sail for America. YOU gambled away your brother's life. And to a *wui!?* You owe this *wui?* You, you should know that now your sister is sailing for Guatemala. You know where this is? Tell me. I had to marry her off to a man leaving for Cuilapa, in Guatemala, who needed a wife. I had to do this because we need the money."

Poor poor Jue Joe. He knew his mother was right. He had always leaned toward risk. He knew that something in him ran a little left, ran a little right. And what risk awaited his sister he didn't know. He knew only that she would land in Mexico and then journey by burrow to the end of the earth. "Cuilapa," sighed aloud Jue Joe. It was a hamlet cleared from jungle that was situated on the west coast of Guatemala. But it was not on any map Jue Joe could find in the general stores of Early California. Instead, he heard about Guatemala from the waggles of merchants in Chinatown's Wui, who exported their goods to Mexico and throughout South America.

After three years working on the San Luis Obispo line, Jue Joe and other Chinese workers were discharged when the Line reached Santa Margarita and when condemnation proceedings in the San Luis Obispo mountains delayed further construction of the Railroad.

Where could he go? Jue Joe caught a stagecoach to Santa Barbara. He squeezed between piles of baggage exposed to wind and rain atop the stagecoach because discrimination prevented him from gaining normal means of travel. And when the stagecoach neared the lower belly of California, Jue Joe hustled for a ticket to ride the southern half of a new railroad route all the way to Chatsworth in the San Fernando valley. He was assigned to a boxcar.

In the Valley, N.C. Johnson and his wife Anne needed help on their large wheat ranch in Chatsworth, and Jue Joe had arrived on the scene at the right time. Yes, agreed the couple among themselves, this Chinaman standing before them was kind of old, but he spoke pretty good English and seemed a sturdy sort. High on their score: the man's countenance projected good manners and he sported a big friendly smile. So, the job of a "China Boy" will be his.

I can tell you that Jue Joe wasn't schooled in cleaning house, doing laundry, taking care of young children, and cooking meals—but he learned quickly and made himself a pretty good semblance of a manservant. What's more, the pay was better than picking grapes or laying railroad ties and he got room and board as well! But big dreams, big dreams that extended way beyond the confines of the Johnson's Chatsworth house howled round Jue Joe's interior. For the land is what called him. The land meant *everything* to Jue Joe. He wanted a farm of his own. And potatoes would make his fortune, harked idea from his inner landscape. For Old China slid a dream down the spine of Jue Joe. His courage came from ancients in the Jue clan (or "Zhao" in Mandarin) whose members were farmer-warriors in the Fen River Valley of Shanxi Provence, in North Central China. Farming was a skill honed sharp during the Warring States Period when vast lands of his ancestors were part of the Yellow River Basin. But how Jue Joe's Clan came to settle in Sum Gong Village in the southern bowel of Guangdong Province is another story.

That was then, this is now.

The year 1893 welcomed Jue Joe's excitement. He had saved enough cash to lease land for his spud farm. Or so he thought. Turns out he had to take a train to Sacramento to get a "dog-tag" card that all Chinamen were forced to have on their person. It was a mean-spirited strike on Chinese by a dominant white culture of the period. The Geary Act had passed, requiring only Chinese in the United States to carry a photo ID card on their person to prove that they were legally in the Country. All Chinese had to show their dog-tags at any time if requested. Jue Joe had gotten a previous Identity Card when he worked in St. Helena, but it did not have his photo on it. As a result, he had to go to Sacramento where his records were held and prove that he was who he said he was to get a new photo ID. Jue Joe booked himself a Fourth-Class train ticket that landed him on a wooden bench in a freight car.

He rode this way from Sacramento back to Chatsworth with no windows in his freight car, and only a sliding door to open for a little fresh air. As the train pulled into Lancaster Station in the Mojave Desert, Jue Joe on impulse hopped to the ground to poke around a bit. He had heard that Lancaster had cheap land for lease, and even though it seemed a barren desert, it had enough water to irrigate his dream of a spud farm, so churned his interior engine.

A rare creek caught the Chinaman's eye. Its cool flow satisfied Jue Joe's parched lips. A few Joshua trees loitered round this rivulet and told Jue Joe that Lancaster would grow. In that instant he saw a tree move. No, no, it was bigger, taller, and it moved closer.

"Howdy, said the tall white man with elfin ears as he shot Jue Joe an easy grin. "Will you share some of that water?"

Sunset sliced the sky a mango red as the Chinaman returned a smile to this striking man with elfin ears. Jue Joe made way for the white stranger at this rivulet. And as a moon climbed up slabs of air, and old stars gathered to dance across the sky, Otto F. Brant began to tell his life's story to Jue Joe. Together the two men built a campfire in the cold desert night.

"I was born in Ohio in 1860," said Otto to his new friend. "That makes me four years younger than you." Like his Chinese companion, Otto had had to make his own way in his youth. His father had died early, and as a result, his family fingered air in an emptied moola jar. So, Otto found himself working in a shoe cobbler's kiosk. From there he morphed into a telegraph operator for the railroad industry and climbed to the position of a station manager. Not bad. He made a bold move, too. He got married. The father of his new wife Susan had made money in California before her family returned to Ohio. Naturally, Otto borrowed $30,000 from his father-in-law. With that cushion, it sparked a dream. With his wife Susan, his younger brother Byron Brant, and himself, the congress set out for Texas to grow their dream. Soon Otto and Byron parlayed the $30,000 loan into $500,000 by building a water irrigation business in Waco, Texas. Then the trio made their way to California to plant new dreams. Byron went to Ontario to start his citrus farm, and Otto and his wife Susan made their way to Los Angeles in which Otto began to buy and sell real estate.

That's when innovation steals forward. Otto F. Brant realized that with conflicts over title to land among buyers in Los Angeles, forming a title insurance company to ensure legal rights to real property would be a damned good hustle. Otto and his co-partners formed the first title insurance company in Greater Los Angeles called "Land Title and Trust Company." He and his partners rode a property boom in the Los Angeles area. To be sure, several years of wet weather in Los Angeles, and hey, Otto's eyes grew to cartoon size on what could be done for a parched San Fernando Valley. A train trip to Lancaster had given him idea toward expanding his title insurance and real estate business. Especially, into the crescent-shaped gem parked in the shadow of Los Angeles—the San Fernando Valley. But a steady flow of water for agriculture to pump alive that hidden gem was his main concern, and he wasn't quite sure if the good times would last. This is why Otto had come to Lancaster, and now, meeting Jue Joe at this creek, well, what a nice surprise. Soon enough his entrepreneur's mind locked onto water of the kind to change San Fernando Valley's character.

Jue Joe could see in Otto's nature that he sported an eye for sources of water that could grow a very big dream.

On this point I will digress. The tale of these two wanderers in the Mojave Desert is revealing of the word "character." Otto was not a man who took to differences in class or race or foreign origin on which to judge a fellow. Instead, Otto embraced the old school of learning. Meaning that he opted to read a fellow's character like a desert varmint does before a strike. He was shrewd; he was empathetic; he was a man of great depth.

Once, Otto F. Brant travelled by train to Yuma, Arizona, which is located by the Colorado River. He was looking to invest in land that his wealthy business cronies in Los Angeles had told him about. They offered to roam with Otto in Yuma. "No," said Otto, "but thank you for your kindness." For he knew that the only way to know your land was to spend time on it; to sleep in the open under the stars. You had to spend time, too, with those who had lived there for generations and who really knew the land and its ways deeply. And so, in the the Yuma Desert, Otto hired Indian guides to help navigate him across his new adventure. He spent time on the land listening intently to what his Indian guides brought up about the land as well.

You could say that Otto knew the character of a Chinaman, too, he learned a little about Chinese culture. It began when he hired a Chinese manservant to help his wife with their brood of six children. For the Brant family enjoyed an active lifestyle in their big home situated in a nice part of Los Angeles.

"Wong Joe," was the manservant's name. "China Boy," was Wong Joe's acknowledged, informal title. But he was no boy, I tell you, he was a grown man who was a trusted member of the Brant family and who raised not only Otto's children, but many of the neighbor's little rugrats as well.

Jue Joe saw in his new friend the following: Otto F. Brant was different from other Lo-fan men whom he had met in America. Otto treated Jue Joe not as a master, and he a servant. No, no, this white soul talked to Jue Joe like an equal. He was a kindred spirit because the two men were dreamers who dreamed big dreams. Similar dreams.

And so, Otto threw away his own First-Class ticket on the train back to Los Angeles, and instead, he joined Jue Joe in Fourth-Class and sat with him on a single bench in a converted freight car to continue their conversation. Rolling back along the rails to the San Fernando Valley and the City of Angels beyond, the two compatriots shared their views about the good earth, about how to grow their dreams on it, and about how people—of the best kind—can be persuaded to help make these dreams happen.

In later years, Jue Joe often told his children that everything he knew about American business—he learned from Otto F. Brant. For Otto was his mentor in how to navigate the complexities of doing business in America. To Jue Joe, his white friend was like a guardian angel to an immigrant newcomer as himself who, lacking in formal education, struggling daily to overcome constraints that grew intense with more

Exclusion Laws passed against Chinese, well, it was a blessing to have this friend from the mainstream world.

Through his Land Title Insurance and Trust Company, Otto arranged for Jue Joe to lease forty-acres of prime land in the Chatsworth area for sowing spuds. And Jue Joe enriched that earth with Old World tilling reconceived for a new world.

In turn, Jue Joe worked for Otto F. Brant to help the latter realize a far-sighted prospect: the ditty of buying and selling land, and for certain, insuring each of those land titles with clear ownership for the buyer. This was creative, assessed Jue Joe's canny. He marvelled at Otto's ability to succeed with oddball dreams when other men didn't think to go the mile to do so.

You might ask at this point what could an illiterate Chinaman do for a rich white businessman in his real estate business?

Let me tell you a tale to help you understand.

R.H. Lloyd, attorney in real property law, stared intently at a Chinese potato farmer perched at the other side of his polished, mahogany desk. The Chinaman had just offered to buy ten-acres of land in the Rancho Portero Felipe Lugo tract that Lloyd's client, E.G. Baldwin, had subdivided years before for the asking price of $1750 dollars. Much to Lloyd's astonishment, the Chinese potato farmer plucked from his dusty breast pocket—a few gold coins. He drew a handful more from the pant pocket of his worn-thin Khaki pants. He spread all his shiners on the desk before R.H. Lloyd, attorney-at-law. And in silence the Chinaman flashed to Lloyd an affable smile. Then his crooked little finger nudged those golden bits a little closer to Lloyd. And to that white man, this Chinaman leaned forward to crack him the biggest, teethy grin from ear to ear.

The instant brought to Lloyd's interior a thing he felt about Chinese: they work nonstop from dawn to dusk in fields growing whatnots, they do this and then squirrel their profits away to a bank, leaving the stash there to collect interest. These Chinamen live in rudimentary shacks, observed R.H. Lloyd, they seem to have no women or children with them to support, and they eat what they can grow on their leased land. Their expenses are minimal, and as result, these Chinamen can outbid white folks to buy our land. What kind of... (expletive deleted) ...are they doing to us!?

But R.H. Lloyd kept his unease to himself; instead, he shook hands with Jue Joe and accepted this potato farmer's gold coins.

Jue Joe's next stop was to visit Mr. H.A. Church and his wife Jeannie who were living on the same ten-acres of land that he had just bought! The couple had fallen on hard times. In 1887 they had bought this land for $850 dollars. But six years later they received notice that the property had reverted to the original subdivider, E.G. Baldwin, for non-payment of mortgage fees for several months and they were being evicted. The Churches contested Baldwin's action in court because they had not been given enough notice. In addition, they claimed that they should still own the property, having made regular payments until the last few months. But in their hearts, the Churches knew that they could not afford the payments even if they won their case.

Enter a strange Chinaman who offered to buy the Church's title of ownership to this property, knowing that E.G. Baldwin had claimed the couple no longer owned that property. It was a quickie. Mr. H.A. Church and his wife Jeannie accepted the stranger's gold coins and signed over their title to the man. Then they dropped their case against E.G. Baldwin and shot out of town.

"That poor, poor Chinaman," blew H.A. Church under his breath to his wife, "the joke's on him. He just bought our worthless acres."

Of course, you should know, the whole deal was set up by Otto F. Brant. As President of Land Title Insurance and Trust, Otto knew that the contested property between Baldwin and the Churches was under "Color of Title." Meaning unclear ownership; a defect exists that makes the property nontransferable. So, he had fronted cash to Jue Joe to buy the property from both Baldwin and the Churches on the same day to clear title and vest uncontested title in Jue Joe, who was then free to sell this property to anyone who wanted to buy it for a nice profit.

Of course, this can be construed as "insider knowledge" to buy and sell property for the benefit of oneself, banters Otto F. Brant's inner shores. So, my friend Jue Joe is the perfect business partner, rings a bell in Brant's interior. Jue Joe is completely trustworthy and loyal. I know this man; I know his character. What's more, he need not know how to read any legal documents. He could just be told where and when to show up to sign his name to seal the deal.

Overnight Jue Joe became a successful potato farmer and a wheeler-dealer of real estate, earning enough dough to finally return home at the ripe old age of forty-six to find himself a wife. The year was 1902.

And now, now in 1906 Jue Joe found himself back in the San Fernando Valley. He was farming again. As I have said to you earlier, Jack, he pole-vaulted into his second act as in the following:

Returning to America had not been easy for Jue Joe. The anti-Chinese immigration laws were strict, and Jue Joe did not have the proper return documents for re-entry into America. He was still considered a Chinese laborer who had "over-stayed" his allowed time of one year in China. As a result, Jue Joe was ineligible to return. But he had friends in high places. His buddies Otto F. Brant and Harry Chandler of the *Los Angeles Times* newspaper pulled some strings for Jue Joe, and he was immediately "landed" in America. Then, Otto helped Jue Joe get back on his feet, arranging for one of his friends to hire old Joe as a houseboy. This was followed by helping Jue Joe lease land in the San Fernando Valley to restart his potato farming business.

Otto introduced Jue Joe to his hired strongman Mr. Thompson. Thompson was rough-looking: he could storm thick muscles at you lickety-split. He bounced squatters off Brant's land deals. But Thompson is of good character, assessed Jue Joe, the bull is trustworthy. So, Jue Joe partnered with Thompson to open a saloon located at 2nd and Broadway in Downtown Los Angeles. Thompson used his skill to bounce soused barflies into a back alley parked behind their saloon. To be sure, Jue Joe wore his Colt.44 M1878 sidearm always strapped to his waist. Moreover, the corner saloon beckoned patrons from its intersection diagonal to the *Los Angeles Times* newspaper building, so *Times'* patrons joined in a tipsy after a hard day's work: inside the mowzy din, Jue Joe knew each man's favorite bracer and had their specialties lined up on the counter ahead of arrival. This is what my father San Tong Jue recalled as if it were only yesterday.

By 1918, Jue Joe's potato farming business had gotten so big that, at the end of harvest season, he was shipping close to 2,000 sacks of potatoes at six dollars a sack from San Fernando Valley to the wholesale warehouse in Downtown Los Angeles.

Still, Jue Joe liked to live a simple life; he liked his dirt-floor cabin. It was here that he came to bear upon Leong Shee's letter to him and ponied up the dough to bring his family to America. I should point out that by this time Jue Joe had become a "merchant," and was a member of a rare, privileged class of Chinamen who could sail family across the blue and into the means of Gold Mountain; and "Gold Mountain" refers to the gold strike of 1849 in California, which flicked villagers' eyes cartoon-size with bold dreams.

The old man sat in his cabin pondering the end of a solitary life. He had not seen his family in decades, and now, he tried to recover their images from memory. He could not. Instead, the old sojourner could only hear babies bawling faintly in a dreamscape, and a young woman breastfeeding to silence them. That's how old his sons were when he had sailed for California in 1906. And now, his two sons would be teenagers. Uh, oh. And of his wife Leong Shee? He had only a silhouette of her moving round his kitchen in shadow play. How would she be now?

Excitement and a little fear slid down Jue Joe's countenance. He consulted his young friend Oliver, now a prosperous attorney. Could a sailing be done? Oliver had worked for Jue Joe as a migrant on his farm in the San Fernando Valley. When Jue Joe saw this white lad in a barn reading law books every night by a hurricane lamp, he sent Oliver to law school to realize the migrant's dream of becoming an attorney, he paid for Oliver's education. This is because Jue Joe valued education, even though it was beyond his own reach. He saw that Oliver had an inner drive and intellectual curiosity that soared beyond the dusty fieldwork the lad had chosen to earn enough money for law studies. Oliver was born poor like Jue Joe had been. So, with Jue Joe's help, Oliver completed his law degree, and he married the daughter of the founder of California Bank.

I tell you that Oliver never forgot Jue Joe's generosity, and he always honored the Chinaman's oral request for a loan from his father-in-law's California Bank to see him through a harvest. The young man never judged this Chinaman as an illiterate who could not read or write; instead, Oliver knew that an oral promise from Jue Joe to repay his loan on time was as good as a signed contract.

And that is how Oliver mapped out the legal route for Jue Joe's family to emigrate to America. He formulated the necessary papers for entry into California, and with those papers in hand, Jue Joe padded down to Los Angeles' Chinatown to hire a letter writer to translate from English into Chinese, the swirls of dots and dashes and legal whatnots penned by Oliver.

CHAPTER 5 – ASPARAGUS OPERA

The *SS Columbia* pulled into San Francisco's view. Leong Shee, now thirty-three-years old, lumbered slowly down the towering Ship's narrow ramp with San You and Song Tong trailing behind her. Each boy—donned in a Buster Brown suit—balanced a heavy cloth bag on his shoulder; they sported billed caps, hip-length jackets, knickers, knee-high socks, and snake shoes with metal taps. A stopover in Hong Kong had given the trio time to buy Western gear to mark their entrance into 1918 America.

"...and they made such a noise," recalled San Tong Jue. Dinner had ended in the family room of our big house on the Jue Joe Ranch, and he continued, "On Angel Island our tap shoes click-clacked on the floorboard of our barrack. We were tight as sardines and the barrack's walls, I assure you, exploded with feeling. The walls erupted with grievances, graffiti, and moody poems. I remember my first draw of the barrack's air, too, clouds of urine snapped my nose. There was so much snoring at night that I could not sleep well. But all the same, the fifty or more men cramped inside our small barrack knew my brother and me by our tap shoes.

"I discovered that we had only three small washbasins for fifty-plus Chinese in our barrack to share, which meant that a good number of the men didn't bother to wash up and which meant that my brother and I wished that we had packed in our cloth bags—nose clips.

"I'm getting ahead of myself, so let me backup. Aboard the *SS Columbia* steamer I run to the top deck of our Ship and see a city like I never imagined: tall buildings hitched together that ran the length of a waterfront. I saw pedestrians clutch their overcoats, too, their heads casting for cover from the wind and chill. Some women scampered across the wharf's clapboards in high-buckled shoes and didn't look up at us on the deck as I waved down at them. I remember that folks leaned into this early March wind that scattered newsprint down a boardwalk. I tucked that image deep in me so that I would always remember my first glimpse of America. What an adventure, I felt. What magic.

"In that instant my mother tapped my shoulder, and her words filled my ear, 'This is San Francisco—but we're heading out there. Can you see that point?' She fingered toward a rock that rippled in the distance. It was across the bay a bit. Then a skipper powered his paw at my mother, my brother, and me to disembark the *SS Columbia* and to step into a small launch that sputtered us toward that rock called "Angel Island."

"When the launch docked at Angel Island, my mother was whisked away from my brother and me. We had no permission to see her, or to communicate with her, for the whole time that we were on Angel Island Immigration Station. We watched our mother being taken to a women's dorm up a hillside. She turned once to look back for us. Then she vanished. My brother and me were assigned a men's barrack at dockside, far below our mother's barrack.

"You ask me, 'What did I eat?' I got a bowl of rice, a piece of salted fish, and one piece of bok choy. That was all. Only two meals a day. So, my brother and me, we get friendly with a kitchen helper who stroked his chin that folded like blankets. The plump said he been camping on this rock for years and never seen a cable car. He told us we might not see one either. Then his face fell, his pitch switched higher, '…and if you get bounced back to China you contact my family in Zhongshan County. That's near Sum Gong Village, you kids. Tell'em I'm a chef in a fine restaurant.' Then he piloted my brother and me into a toilet stall and whispered, 'You fathah rich? You eat better in kitchen with me. You tell him slip me three dollah every week and you eat good with me in kitchen.' He was a plucky card with not a bone protruding that you could see, so we smuggled a note to our mother, and she in turn smuggled word to our father who was, she replied through some lady's calligraphy, in San Francisco's Chinatown burning his guts to spring us."

It was May 2, 1918, on Angel Island. A bungalow's window shade was dawn. Inside that dim sanctum a bare lightbulb suspended from the ceiling flared awake. It lobbed its glare on a man fidgeting with his lapel. Seated on a bentwood chair the man, donned in suit and tie, drummed his crooked little finger on his thigh. Seated next to Jue Joe was Leong Shee looking stiff as a barrel on her chair; she'd been released from the women's barrack up the hill, and now, she braced herself for a moment of great import.

In quick time a wooden door creaked open, and Leong Shee rose to greet her two sons for the first time in months. The boys stood before their parents under spotlight. For this was the character of the moment. To let go of home and start anew? The return lay in one word. Sacrifice. It was for children to enjoy the full bloom of harvest reaped by hands unearthing unknowns. It was for children to enjoy an education that their parents—focused on production for a new tomorrow—could never enjoy for themselves.

Leong Shee's eyes moistened as she saw San You and San Tong, who were accompanied by a uniformed officer. She nudged her sons forward a bit, and spoke in their ears, "This is your Pa." And she threw her chin up at Jue Joe with pride. Her eyes motioned her husband toward his sons so that he took in her accomplishment: babies that through HER tutelage over the years had morphed into strapping teenagers.

"H'lo Pa," chorused San You and San Tong to the man donned in a Western suit. This caused Jue Joe to crack a very wide smile from ear to ear. Taking each son's hand in his, Jue Joe led his two teenagers into sunny weather and into a forest thick with great unknowns. Leong Shee, on the other hand, paced six feet behind the trio.

San Francisco was Chinatown and all you could eat. It was crab stalls and shops selling curios and noisy drama tacking down Dupont Street (today's Grant Avenue). It was letter writers parked on sidewalks helping bachelors remit funds to their families in the old country. It was rows of bachelor's quarters bent this way and that with wet laundry hanging from bamboo poles attached to balconies. It was Chinese scurrying round dirt alleys with their cloth bags filled with wondrous, pungent whatnots. But most important, it was folks clicking in the Pearl River delta's dialect that Leong Shee and her two sons could understand.

Padding down a dusty lane, the four-some stopped at an open kiosk in which ducks were tonged on meat hooks, dripping a sweet-smelling, succulent perfume.

Here, Jue Joe steered his family to a table with stools in that tiny kiosk for a big dim sum lunch; a treat that was very missed by Leong Shee and her two sons while incarcerated on Angel Island Immigration Station for months.

During their meal, San Tong sneaked a side glance at Jue Joe. He registered furrows roiling round Jue Joe's suntanned face. He noted streaks of gray stamped across his father's temples and saw a man, no, no, he saw a "Wanted" poster reeling with rugged will and thunderous ocean. For Jue Joe, at sixty-two-years old, whipped up an image of a seasoned enigma that only dreamers carry on their characters.

Jue Joe, on the other hand, never dreamed of a day like this. Between dumplings and small talk, he studied his sons with keenness. Yes, he recognized bits of himself in them. But what about her? Leong Shee seemed a counterfeit copy of the young girl he had married in Sum Gong Village, back in 1902. Time appeared to have dulled her image and she seemed out of sync with her new surroundings. Could she adopt to life on the Western range? This is California and, well, life can be rough here.

Their tenement building on Ferguson Alley in Old Chinatown, Los Angeles, was a constant assault of streetcars hooting day and night. Above Jue Joe's apartment on the second floor, a balcony on the third floor dripped wet laundry to drown Leong Shee's herbs on her balcony. These were Chinese herbs that were prisoners ensnared like her in a foreign flowerpot. Her humiliation was complete: Gum Saan wasn't supposed to be this way. Lonely tears filled Leong Shee's eye sockets. Two years she bawled before she finally broached Jue Joe with urgency. She begged her husband who was twenty-eight years her senior, "I want to go home. I demand that you send me back home!" And then she threw her chin up and croaked, "Sum Gong Village is a queen compared to this!"

"What!? You dare mouth at me this way? I paid good bucks for you. So, what I say goes. You stay right here, and you will obey ME!" This was prairie talk. This was what a pioneer like Jue Joe, who was a producer of means but not of gentle temperance, this was how he came to treat family relations. For he didn't know any better but to pull rank like an emboldened fart. For Old Los Angeles was dressed like cowboy lore and there was no room for wheezy fussing. You had to be tough as hardtack; a stone-cold cracker that men ate on cattle drives round Old California. They still do in some parts. Jue Joe mixed water and flour, let it dry, and it made for simplicity. He liked his life this way.

A season fired forward, and Leong Shee developed another approach to her ilk: whenever Jue Joe revved his verbal engine at her, she backed off. She defected. In her interior she relocated to China. In his exterior Jue Joe took to educating his boys. He hired a tutor for his two sons, and the lessons of commerce and of the English language entered their youthful minds.

"I entered First Grade, and my school was located on First Street in Downtown Los Angeles," recalled Father. He lowered himself into a wingback chair by the living room's fireplace, and you heard its leather squeak on contact, and you felt the fire's roaring flames fan alive Father's impressions. "My teacher sat me beside her desk," resumed Father's voice, "my eyes were level with her brooch that was pinned to her pleated high collar. It was possibly a donkey, I suppose, and at thirteen-years of age, I felt like a donkey because kids half my age at recess chanted in my face, 'Ching Chong Chinaman….' This hurt me. The same grazing flicked from lips of grownups, too, when I ventured out in public: 'Hey Chink, go back where you….' I asked myself, why do they hate me? Why want me to feel so ashamed of who I am, of my skin, of my culture? It's as if they want me to hate myself, want me to feel dirty inside, and they don't care to know who I really am. There was no answer for an outsider like me, I came to realize, and from then on, I never felt I belonged anywhere but in myself. I studied hard in school, my children, I studied very hard to hold my own worth."

July 1, 1918, was a special day. The boys had been in Los Angeles for one month and they were doing well in their studies. Jue Joe brought them Downtown to Harry Chandler's office at the *Los Angeles Times* newspaper building. Old Joe had become friends with Harry Chandler through his buddy Otto F. Brant. The boys' politeness and command of some English words brought cheers from Mr. Chandler who served as Editor-in-Chief of this major newspaper in that fast-growing Metropolis. "Good god Joe—you did it! You've made educated young men of your boys," exclaimed Harry Chandler, flashing a grin at Jue Joe's sons San You and San Tong. Then he poured for each of the trio a glass of seltzer water with ice.

"The seltzer felt refreshing on such a hot day," evokes San Tong's youth. "I'd never tasted American soda pop before. The soda that you know today, kids, they weren't invented yet. So, seltzer water was a big thing." The trio had taken a streetcar that dropped them off in front of the *Times* building. The Red Car was filled with characters in all sorts of dress. It was stifling, too, being stuffed in the back of the Car, as Chinese were not allowed to sit anywhere up front.

San Tong smiled as another yesteryear stole into view. "Although it took some getting used to, chocolate candy was an item I slowly got used to. At first, it tasted bitter to me. This is because in China we ate only oranges and other fruits for dessert. But Mr. Chandler offered my brother and me chocolate candy. So, I accepted his kind offer and thought how strange the American diet."

"After giving us a tour of the news operation, Harry Chandler led the three of us up to the rooftop of the *Times* building where I caught a view of a miniature city below. I'm speaking of the old *Times* building, not the new one that you see today. Harry Chandler posed us in front of two brick pillars that were elevator shafts, and I remember that one pillar had a pair of eagle's wings set on top as if poised for flight. At once he had his photographer snap our picture and we became a real story in the *Los Angeles Times*. I sure felt proud of my father! I learned that Pa was a well-known man around Los Angeles, and I've kept that news clipping all these years."

The text of the July 1, 1918, newspaper article reads:

"United after a separation of more than a dozen years, one of the happiest families in Los Angeles today is that of Jue Joe, well-known Chinese merchant and marketman. A few days ago, Jue Joe's two sons and their mother arrived from the province of Sun Wai, China. Jue Sun You is 15 years old, and Jue Sun Tong is 13. Jue Joe had not seen them nor his wife since the youngest boy was four months old. The lads were immensely pleased at the prospect of coming to America, and although they knew not a single word of English when they sailed, they at once applied themselves to learning the language, and each can now write many words in English and they have quite an extensive vocabulary. Jue Joe has employed a tutor for them, and they have their English lessons daily. His ambition is to give them training in the American schools and make good American businessmen of the lads. Jue Joe plans soon to make a thorough inspection of the lands in Imperial Valley with the idea of forming a Chinese company for extensive farming in that region." -- *Los Angeles Times,* July 1, 1918.

How the trolleys ran up and down Temple Street in Downtown Los Angeles! These electrical marvels took Father everywhere. What's more, the "Red L" streetcar, well, it was magical that such a wooden marvel could toot you from Downtown LA to the San Fernando Valley, and then across the Valley's endless fields to drop you a day's walk to Jue Joe's potato farm in Chatsworth, which was an old stagecoach stop situated at the far northeast corner of the Valley.

"Witmer, Witmer!" shrieked a conductor who shoved a brass switch forward. By a miracle the skinny door of the Big Red trolley lurched open. "Last stop ... end of the line ... Witmer Street," he shouted.

In the rear of the Big Red's "L Line" two lads remained glued to their wooden seats. This prompted the conductor with his glove hooked to a bell strap to whip that strap wildly. The sound exploded two boys off their seats and their tap shoes took to the floorboard to reach the front of the Car.

"Widmah?" queried San You at the white conductor. The uniformed man winced.

"Yeah, yeah," shot the worn voice hidden beneath his oversized uniform. Not a smile split the man's face as he peered through the thickest spectacles you ever saw; it made his eyes look like zippers. Lucky for the lads, however, the man wasn't battle-hardened like some municipal folks. It was only that he felt tired of repeating his stops, especially into the ear-horns of elderly biddies who pumped at him, 'Eh?' He skimmed more than one hour from Downtown Los Angeles to the San Fernando Valley's fruit stands for those biddies, repeating each stop like a stuck record.

"Witmer!" exclaimed the conductor to San You and San Tong. The boys watched the man's index finger point to a street that stretched before them. San You and San Tong began their slog down Witmer Street, aiming for Chatsworth in the northwest face of the San Fernando Valley. They padded for hours to find Jue Joe's potato farm installed somewhere in Chatsworth's most remote corner. They followed Witmer Street until it became a dirt wagon trail, they followed the wagon trail until it became a cow's meander, and down they ribboned through swirls of sagebrush and mustard weeds until, by golly, an entire day brought them into sunset and to Jue Joe's potato farm. This, according to San Tong Jue's recollection.

Eighty acres of a potato farm loomed before San You and San Tong. Eighty! This was impressive to the boys. For Jue Joe had not informed them about its metes and bounds. Only that there was a bunkhouse where they could stay overnight if they could find the farm.

Inside Jue Joe's bunkhouse there was no faucet, no water, and no toilet. The Redwood barrack had ten beds stacked five high on each side of the one-room shack.

There was no heat, noted the boys, and you felt the night's deep-freeze. Eight Chinese working stiffs that night in Jue Joe's bunkhouse and the boys made ten. Ten workers and Jue Joe and only one oil lamp to share if anyone needed to take a leak outside in frigid forecast. This was life spare as a varmint's; this was a throwback to the old country.

Night drew slowly away at 4:00 A.M. and working stiffs began to stir. Kerosene-coffee, at least that's how it tasted, shot the men awake. After downing rice porridge, the men let their calf-high boots march them into Jue Joe's potato field; there, it was stooped labor for the stiffs until the sun yawned asleep. Ten horses tacked the workers down rows of Jue Joe's field. Ten brown mares with their black tails snapping side to side and they were harnessed to wooden plows that cut endless avenues of future revenue. It was a race among farmers in the San Fernando Valley to ride the food wagon of progress for a blossoming America.

"O beautiful for spacious skies, for amber waves of grain ... *(oogah!)* ... above the clouds so high. America, America...." ('Crank the cars—we're in a hurry!') ... "Over there, over there, and the Yanks are coming, the Yanks are coming...." ('Shadup Woodrow Wilson!')

In 1918 Jue Joe's taters joined a war. He moved boxcars of potatoes by rail to Uncle Sam's soldiers on the frontline of battle. World War I had engulfed America's fighting best in a European beef, which in no time multiplied round the world. No major nation had escaped the fray. Jue Joe's ten horses kicked their manes up and forward like a steam locomotive chugging taters to market. But they were no match—not one and not all—against a sleek, Pierce-Arrow Town Car that Jue Joe unleashed upon his field. Why that flivver ran 124-horsepower under its hood! The 5-passenger stud was black and shiny and had two crystal lamps to sharpen your way through a dystopian world that seemed bereft of reason. In the chauffeur's carriage of the Pierce-Arrow, a talking horn inlaid with mother-of-pearls shot its cord through glass to link Jue Joe to his driver. The Pierce-Arrow's red-velvet seats sported tufts like crown jewels too. Clearly, the Car made itself known as a loud piece of action. Indeed, the rolling Beast had idea of its own. Its engine revved as ropes tied to its fender strained to divest the earth of tree stumps and bumps. That's how Jue Joe's iron Beast worked his potato farm in Chatsworth for the War effort.

"Pa always wore calf-high boots," pressed Father's recall. "I remember that they were always mud-caked right up to his boot's top laces. And around Pa's waist hung his keys, the kind that projected one tooth. Those keys sounded off as he moved; so, you always knew when he was coming."

That's how my father brought Jue Joe to life for me, Jack. Clips of my father's old life revealed the terrain that he had to walk through. He learned that Jue Joe's intellect was sharp as a machete. The old man honed his photographic memory because he couldn't read or write. He worked round his deficit through use of association; raised it to the level of art. Meaning that he would attach a thing unusual about a person he met to remember that person or an event.

"I was scared of Pa because if you crossed him—he made you sorry," said my father San Tong. "The old man couldn't stand failure—especially in his own sons. He took perfection to be the only course for my brother San You and me. And need I say? You delivered yourself to Pa in the Chinese way, or else. Filial piety was drilled into us. Pa was as intricate as spit gears and locks. However, he dressed in a manner plain and simple. He didn't want noth'in fancy except for that Pierce-Arrow Town Car. Pa owned only one suit. And he wore that suit only once for a family photograph. I think the year was 1924. My brother and me begged him for days to pose with us for that one and only family photo taken together: Pa and Ma, my brother and me, and Corrine and Dorothy. The rest of the time Pa lived in his khakis. He wore khakis and never washed them for days. I take that back. He wore clean khakis when he beat to the bank for loans. 'Simplicity,' he used to say to me, 'keeps you focused on what you really gotta do in life.'

"One day Pa said to me, 'Nothing lasts forever but this here earth, son, you gotta invest in it. You gotta live for it in your soul.' I can remember the day we entered the California Bank. Pa's mind squirreled off like an abacus, he had calculated a loan amount in his head before we even saw his friend Oliver. You see, Oliver was a lawyer at his father-in-law's California Bank. And Oliver was the man who had sent my mother, my brother, and me ninety pages to memorize before our ship landed in San Francisco. This was back in 1918. Maybe I've told you this before, I don't remember.

"When Pa and I entered Oliver's office, the young man's blue eyes lit up with real joy. I remember Oliver smoothing back his blond hair as he rose from a big leather chair behind a mahogany desk. He gave us each a bear hug. I'm thinking, this guy's honest looking. I liked Oliver immediately.

"An overhead light in his office flicked a little, and I saw a face more advanced than his thirty-years of age, though he was only that. Oliver looked a bit ghostly, he looked kinda fragile in health, his eyes seemed otherworldly. It hit me as odd that on his mahogany desk, Oliver switched his desk lamp to 'high' just to sign a bank draft for Pa. Daylight filtering through a picture window in his office seemed bright enough to me.

"Afterward, I roared Pa to Imperial Valley in our pickup truck. He had in mind to lease another ranch in Indio, which is in the Imperial Valley of Southern California. Bouncing on the worn front seat Pa folded Oliver's bank draft in half and ran his yellow thumbnail down its back to pinch it tight. Opening his chained watch to check our progress Pa turned to me and said, 'Oliver not like others on ranch before your time. He work hard in field and read books at night on potato sacks he make for bed. I say, 'Oliver what you read?' 'Law,' he say. No money for study so he come to ranch to work for me. I say to Oliver, 'You good boy, you go school. I pay. No pay me back, o.k.?' And that's how Oliver, at twenty-four-years old, graduated from law school with highest honors.

"Pa continued to tell me the story, 'He marry girl whose father is founder of California Bank; fella by name of W.A. Grant. I think her father had made his money in railroads somewhere in the Southwest.' Oliver remained grateful to Pa all these years. A loyal friend, he was like a member of our family."

Seven-hundred acres of Mr. Anderson's barley field is up for grabs. It was part of the Gardiner Wallace Dickey Ranch rolling with Kansas grain and sugar beets. Mr. Dickey had purchased that seven-hundred acres from the I.N. Van Nuys Ranch and had subdivided the land into what is called "West Van Nuys." But there's more. Today, the incorporated City of Van Nuys can trace its origin back to the original Rancho Encino. In fact, all the above ranches that I mentioned can. It's a long chain of titles that lead you back to Mexican land grants of yesteryear; the San Fernando Valley was dotted with rancho this and rancho that. And new communities grew from that rich adobe life.

Now, in Jue Joe's saloon at Second and Broadway, Otto F. Brant watched Walter Mendenhall of the California Land and Development Company swig a shot of rye. Retired from the rag-and-print trade, Walter Mendenhall had passed his Van Nuys Publishing Company called *"The Valley News and Greensheet"* to his heirs. He was now on the Commission of the West Van Nuys Subdivision.

"Hey Walt, gimme the lowdown on the Anderson parcel's value," nudged Otto F. Brant to Walter Mendenhall. He bought Walter another shot of rye. "This is important, Walt. You see, we could do some business together and…."

"Subdivision, Joey! Didn't I tell you so? Didn't I tell you that this whole Valley was gonna blow open? Here's your chance," pumped Otto to his friend Jue Joe. "Buy into it now, Pal, what can you lose? If needed, I'll loan you cash like you did for me when I was starting out."

The Title Insurance and Trust Company that Otto F. Brant cofounded in Los Angeles would become the largest title company in the nation.

"Now I know Sacramento has passed that Alien Land Law so you people born abroad can't own any land here," continued Otto. "But I'll buy the land for you in my

Title Company's name and hold it in trust for your American-born daughters who are US citizens. They can legally take title when they come of age. Then I'll transfer your land back to you through them. I'll swing the deal—cut around corners—consider it done insurance and all, my friend."

With the Anderson parcel dropping to $240 per acre in the San Fernando Valley's baby year of 1919, Jue Joe put up $24,000 for one-hundred acres of the Anderson property; mind you, in the year of 1919 Jue Joe's first-born daughter Corrine was born in Los Angeles. In time, West Van Nuys would be known as "Tract 1000." And Tract 1000 was subdivided by Otto F. Brant into the cities of Van Nuys, Marion (later known as "Reseda"), and Owensmouth (later known as "Canoga Park").

At once Jue Joe's asparagus ranch in Van Nuys just north of the Sepulveda Reservoir turned lush hues of green. Its character lit the sky with a big dream as machetes clipped green spears and overnight those gems slept in boxcars rolling across a young America. Over the Rockies and beyond the Great Plains—from Portland to Denver to Chicago; from Detroit to New York and Maryland—Jue Joe's boxcars fed America's insatiable appetite. It took Jue Joe five years to wean an asparagus shoot to make it ready for market. Then, these tender spears would clone itself for years and didn't drain the soil like potatoes did every three years.

Oliver with his law books who loved a lady and left no heirs no stamp of himself on the globe died of leukemia at the age of thirty-two. Jue Joe wept when he heard the news.

"Hear me, Joe?" drifted a gentle vapor in Jue Joe's dream. That night he recognized the voice of Oliver. "What you want can't be yours, Joe, not ever in your name. You can't even make a will and give your land to whom you want because the law says it is not yours to give. You are a Chinaman born in a foreign land and that means you are worth nothing in the eye of American jurisprudence. It's all about pedigree, Joe. And you haven't got it here. I'm so sorry for you. Some folks learn to work life their way, call it breaks I guess, and some do not. I fear for you because you can't fight what's coming on the horizon and I can't be there to fight it for you. But I truly love you, Joe, remember that. I wish for you and your family the best." Jue Joe roiled awake soaked in sweat.

The photo of Father's family is remarkable. I have included it on the cover of this book. It is the only image of Jue Joe caught with the pack. Seated on a chair he wears his only suit washed and pressed. Age and weather hack across his face. To me he looks like a gladiator with skill to master the wounds of life. But seated to Jue Joe's left is his wife Leong Shee. She's so young and has something behind her countenance: a hopeful outlook that, alas, has been dumped upon. What inward moves you can catch in a photo. For I see that her ebony hair swings into a bun at the back of her head, its twisted round as so much of her life.

On Leong Shee's lap, well, that's my Aunt Corrine. She's two years older than my Aunt Dorothy. Corrine's expression suggests the need for greater space—hilltop estates preferred. Her pie-shaped face reveals her social yearnings. And there, there on Jue Joe's lap squirms my Aunt Dorothy, a toddler hurling hints of touchiness, her eyes sharp as the crags of the Santa Susana Mountains. It's a wilful glue shooting at you between the eyes—her need to dominate you.

In the back row of this photo, I see Uncle San You who stands at ease. He throws me a broad and confident exterior, like the zest of a debonair. Uncle's features detail our yesteryear's Jue attributes. Meaning the genes of a long face and even proportions. And there's a sense of humor skidding across his face too.

"In the middle of action, that's where I'd always find him," said Father to me about Uncle San You. Or Uncle "Sam" as we Anglicized his name. "My brother told me he planned to fly a Kitty Hawk to Sum Gong Village and land it right in our front yard," continued Father, "he'd gotten his pilot's license the day before our family's photograph was taken."

As Father spoke of his brother, I felt his voice grow heavy, as if feeling out some memory, either between them or around them which was clearly painful, something I was yet to understand. In the back row standing behind Leong Shee is my father shrouded in sepia dreams. I know Father is fourteen years older than Corrine, which makes him sixteen years older than Dorothy, and the emotional distance between them is like father and daughters. He projects a poignant face in this photo that runs the latitude of many rustic feelings. Imagination writes "No Trespass" across his interior landscape, a landscape stamped with very shy meridians. But here's the rub. Father seems destined to shoulder the depth of human wounds, that's what I see. And as I move closer to examine such a hint, I catch his keen inspection of life's flaws. I see what this snapshot of Jue Joe's family means to me. This photo shows us wanting to be a family, struggling for an identity in a strange new land when, in the climate of the times, no identity is allowed for such an entity whose roots begin in China.

Regarding my two aunts in America, I tell you the following: to my aunts came roller skates, talking pictures, indoor plumbing, the speakeasy, the Victrola, and Okeh records. And after graduation from Van Nuys High School, they went on to universities, they enjoyed the laughter and scintillation of America in its quintessence through world wars that gripped America. In other words, my two aunts enjoyed US citizenship!

In contrast, Jue Joe couldn't own a shard of Uncle Sam's clay, nor could San You and San Tong. They were barred by federal and state laws, as I'd mentioned to you earlier.

California's Alien Land Law Act of 1913 could be considered an extension of the federal Chinese Exclusion Law. If under the Chinese Exclusion Law, you could not become a naturalized citizen, then you could not own land in California, nor could you lease its lands for more than three years. I add that only in 1952 was the Alien Land Law Act declared unconstitutional in California on the basis that it prejudiced a particular race; namely, the Chinese and the Japanese.

But for these American minorities the damage to their lives, and to the generations that followed them, was irreparable. Moreover, the irony is that those minorities had helped make California's produce coveted in the global markets of today.

In Jue Joe's case, he had to deed his land holdings to his daughters because they have California birth certificates, having been born on American soil. While in the eyes of the Alien Land Law in California, Jue Joe and his two sons cannot own land for the single reason that they were born in China—and Chinese cannot become US citizens. Now, two sisters hold for two brothers Jue Joe's hard-fought dream to own land on which to realize a future for his family. Imagine underpinnings invoked by that action.

Jue Joe hurt so bad in his stomach that he could not rise from his sheetless bed. Hours passed in his dirt-floor cabin as aroma corkscrewed sweetly up from Jue Joe's pipe, the one with a brass knob protruding from its middle. Each drag on that pipe and a thick paste, dark as molasses, bubbled inside the pipe's knob. Self-reliant in a gilded age Jue Joe doctored his pain in this way: poppy gum. In fact, old-timers did this in the back alleys of Chinatown because, under American law, Chinese were not allowed to seek treatment from white doctors; and hospitals pinned on their doors "white only" signs. As a result, mistrust of that inland world percolated among these groups, and helped to further the practice of opium smoking in hidden crannies.

"If a doctor wants your leg," threw Jue Joe's wind to his son San Tong, "he'll chop it off—like that!" He sliced across his hip and leg joint with one sweep of his paw, signalling to San Tong who'd voiced that they seek help from the inland world.

….and then he moved his family onto the Van Nuys ranch and two homes awaited the family, not just one. Leong Shee and children were assigned to a Redwood cottage that highlighted one central attraction: a jolly black-iron stove. And their twenty-by-forty-foot cottage, according to Father, stood twenty paces away from Jue Joe's abode, which was, and would always be, a one-room earthen cabin. To be sure, Jue Joe's door gave a creak when you opened it. He cut out squares that posed as windows absent of glass, and wooden side-panels with hooks were used to shut the exposed portholes. This was just the way Jue Joe liked to do his thing. With simplicity, as I'd said earlier. He slept among his worn saddles and bridles, which threw a leathery whiff round the room. Daily, he worked with old tools in need of repair. And each night Jue Joe slept with a cleaver under his pillow, for who knows what riffraff loitered round his farm at night. He knew his cleaver could take a nogooder in a *whoosh.*

The old-timer kept his dreams exactly where they fell in his cabin, and Leong Shee received no permit to enter his country. Not even to clean it. To make his point to her: each dawn he chained and padlocked his refuge before departure to his fields. To Jue Joe such action was natural. It was the way of farm folk as he had lived it. But for his two sons? No, no, he had in mind a different track for them. For San You and San Tong must walk a tightrope between two worlds of thought.

I tell you, Jack, Van Nuys High School in the San Fernando Valley revealed to San Tong its allurements. The School disclosed to San Tong its sports events, dances, picnics, school trips to Cornwell's Crystal Plunge on Kester Avenue, which was a public swimming hole, and those doors slammed in his face. These social events were forbidden to sons of China. San Tong was not an "American," deemed oddball choosers in the halls of learning. However, to prove his worth, his patriotism, San Tong threw his heart into R.O.T.C. at Van Nuys High School so that he could advance to West Point.

"At West Point I'll train hard to become an officer," ran San Tong's hanker like a stuck record. He would be a strong leader for his men, he briefed himself, and together they would fight the battles for this nation. San Tong held steadfast to his big dream. He believed in his dream until, one day, his drill instructor informed him that West Point, too, was out of the question for China-born men. And so, science became San Tong's passion.

I tell you that if the halls of ivy had opened just a crack for young San Tong, he would have risen to meet America's call for new scientific research. He wanted to be a researcher in food science and to contribute to this growing field. He felt it in him to push the envelope.

"Your son San Tong has real promise, Joe," said Oliver to the old-timer one day, as the two men paced round the Van Nuys ranch like in days of yesteryear. The young attorney continued, "Why don't you send him to college? He really wants to learn. I had a nice talk with him and—"

"You no see what Chinese see," interrupted Jue Joe, tossing him a bit of sad refrain. "No place for him in American arena. My sons stay home—work on ranch!" To old Joe success is born from tilling the sandy loam for a thrust of treasures. He had this to teach his sons: be a good plant man, be the best. For Jue Joe was the first Asian man to farm in the San Fernando Valley. And naturally, his sons must continue to set a good example in this community comprised mainly of white folk. His sons must show their respect for the good earth. They must show that Chinese can make it on their own—in any community—if they fight hard to realize their dreams and never give up the effort.

What a celebration the San Fernando Valley missed when, in Los Angeles' Chinatown, a wedding foisted on guests all the food that they could eat. Chinese families wheeled toward Spring Street to honor San You and his new bride May Kam. In several restaurants a thousand guests sat at banquet tables chatting and laughing. It was a good moment. Jue Joe had hired limousines and taxis that gunned round Los Angeles to fetch the old-timers. This was Chinese custom. For the old-timers would feign unworthiness at accepting your invitation to dine at such an illustrious occasion. You had to beg them to attend. You had to pick them up at their homes and transport them to the banquet hall to show your respect to these old-timers. And when the ancients were shown to their tables at the wedding banquet, you gifted each one with a rice bowl wrapped in red tissue. This was proper Chinese etiquette.

Jue Joe coughed up a bundle for San You's wedding to May Kam. But he didn't mind because on the Van Nuys ranch he hid alone, inside his one-room cabin. The old man liked his world this way. For him a celebration lay in seeing his rows of asparagus crops coat the Valley green. It lay in feeling Winter's storm powder the San Gabriel Mountains like ice-cream cones. To old Joe, a true day's worth was hearing the sights and sounds and smells of a life well-lived close to the earth. He hoped that his sons and those WHO ARE YET TO BE BORN would one day know this truth. But today, this day, a big celebration for his eldest son in Chinatown's finest restaurants was, well, it was for the benefit of his extended family and his long-time friends.

The joy of San You's marriage, however, was short-lived. It happened suddenly. San You succumbed to leukemia. And no one saw it coming. The old man drove his pickup truck to the Chinese section of Rosedale Cemetery, in Los Angeles, where rows of stand-up slabs marked the end of a brief entity. A slab inscribed with vertical Chinese calligraphy and a gate releasing a dove marked the spirit of San You embedded forever in thick granite; forever exposed to the harsh rhythms of wind and rain. It was here before this slab that Jue Joe sat by his son for hours on end.

If you ask why such things happen and search for answers, you find none. If you seek truth and hear only the wind, you go crazy. Jue Joe could find no answer for the loss of San You, and down his soul, he could feel the loss of his own dreams that could have been.

"What!?" cried Jue Joe, "get outta my house a you!"

My Aunt May had demanded that Jue Joe pony up to support her and her three daughters for the rest of their lives. May Kam was born and raised in America, and from her perspective, such a grievance should fly in your face. To Jue Joe, she had challenged him in a foreign way; impudence cannot be tolerated. No matter how much a parent loves his child, if that child violates a serious taboo, a parent cannot forgive. Proper bearing in matters of death is sacred. In this case, Jue Joe had not been ready to think about money—let alone to pork it over to a woman. Jue Joe was grieving for the apple of his eye—San You who was his first-born son.

So, for Aunt May's bitter verbosity, which to the old man fell toward felony, she was shown the back door. This action caused San Tong and his mother Leong Shee to sneak to May Kam Jue money to meet her needs. The financial support came from their own pockets. Likewise, my brother Jack Sr did the same for May Kam and her three young daughters.

CHAPTER 6 – ROSE AND PING

I want to tell you about my father San Tong Jue's first wife. I never had the pleasure of feeling her hand on mine or seeing her bright smile, but I know her through the memories of her two children, my older brother Jack Sr. and my older sister Joan. They were the only children of Rose Chung Jue. Jack and Joan's mother vanished from their world way too soon. For seven-year-old Jack and five-year-old Joan, their mother Rose's sudden death left a wound felt deep within their souls, a pain that never subsided in their lives. To never feel a mom's loving touch again or to hear her comforting voice, you know, is more than a void in a youngster's life, it is a spiritual vacuum incomprehensible that gnaws without a face at facets of living and beyond, for sure.

Rose's father Thomas Chung was a successful produce merchant in Chinatown, Los Angeles. Often, San Tong would accompany his father Jue Joe on trips Downtown to Thomas Chung's wholesale market. One day, San Tong met Thomas' daughter Rose, and in no time, he became smitten with the beautiful, and very Americanised, Rose Chung. Born in America and immersed in its values, Rose became aware that San Tong had come from a culture steeped in old-world traditions. But as their relationship grew, she taught him to express his feelings openly, enjoy adventures in a new world, in other words, the ways of American culture. However, the young couple married only after San Tong's older brother San You had married May Kam. This was Chinese custom. Family relationships are defined by a hierarchy, and you show respect by adherence to its rules.

My oldest sister Joan kept her mother Rose's letters all these years, and the love letters between San Tong and Rose revealed to us a side of our father that we never knew. To us, he was the stern Chinese father who bared our shortcomings to our faces and expressed his deep love for us by lecturing to us how to do better.

The letters show two young people very much in love. San Tong was nineteen years old; Rose was sixteen years old. Here is Father's letter to Rose when they were dating.

To Rose Chung

3430 Walton Ave.

Los Angeles, California

Van Nuys, Cal.

May 21, 1924

HONEY!

I was disappointed the other day, but this morning your precious letter came and what a welcome it received. I cannot tell you how much it pleased me, and I surmise that it is unnecessary thing for me to mention it, for u probably know, after all this long years of acquaintance, know that I am always delighted to the full measure when I received your letters although the last did not meet my desire of it's length, but I suppose u were in case that I am in now, having little to write about. Nevertheless it certainly was a nice letter and I hope in a near future I shall have the pleasure of receiving another one with the sweet words of my sweet old Gal.

In reading over your letter, especially where the jokes are, it reminds me of something I know:

If there aren't any women in this world we wouldn't be here,

But if there aren't any men in this world,

the women will be as lonesome as I am sitting here.

So after all, the men are quite important too. Once the sweet Sixteen said (perhaps this is my makeup)

"O, you sweet chili-con carne, hot-tamale!!!!!!

You are the sweetest thing in the world

If u come near to me, I'll down on my knees.

If u come closer to me, I shall be at very ease

If you come still closer to me, I begin

So O come!, O come! Sweet man.

Just one more before you leave my hands."

Well that's pretty good ain't it? I shall try to come out to tell you some more. I only regret that you can not go out with me alone. I know how difficult it is to have fun when one goes out, with old people act as…what you may call. Anyway I'll try to come out.

(signed) SANTONG

Now they are married. Here is Rose's letter to my father when he was away farming with Grandpa Jue Joe in Indio, California. It is Thanksgiving and she is pregnant with "Ah Yit," my older brother Jack. "Ah Yit" means number one or first-born in Chinese.

Los Angeles, Nov 25, '27

Dearest Husband,

Am writing a few lines to know how you are getting along. Are you working hard, and do you miss me very much? I sure miss you, Honey Boy!! We thought perhaps you were coming back for Thanksgiving Day. Sam phoned the nite before saying that he would bring a turkey and a couple of chickens out the following day. ("Sam" refers to San You.) So we did have turkey, dressing, potatoes, chicken, Birds nest soup and Roast pork. It was good! Oh, how I wished you were here to eat it with us!! It didn't taste near as good as it would have if you were with us too!

Gee, I'd like to bring you folks some turkey, cause I'd know you'd like it! But just think of the distance, 150 miles to go and 150 miles back. I'd like to take the train but the distance I'd have to walk!!! Oh Baby! when are you coming back to "Ah Yit" and me? You've been gone five whole days already!! Sometimes I get so lonesome I cry.

I went up town and got myself a hat. I hope you like it. I got it down at Bullock's. I got Ma a hat for her birthday. I told her "I'm going to spend $5 on you anyway, so you might as well choose what you like, before I buy something you don't care for!! So she chose a hat. I bought Dad a wool shirt for $4. I brought the clock to fix and they're going to charge me $1.50 for fixing it. I'm going to buy $5 of yarn to knit a blanket. After I buy that, I'll sure be broke!

Isn't it funny how fast money goes?

Mother wants to know how Father is and if he is any better. Please give him my regards. Mother hasn't been so well either, backache, headache, heartache and etc. I told her to let me bring her to the doctors but she says the doctor doesn't do much good anyway. Sometimes she's alright but at other times she doesn't feel good at all. Just like me! Sometimes I'm alright but gee, sometimes my back hurts me terrible, also my tummy feels so heavy. I guess it's "Ah Yit". Gee! I'd be glad if I was all through with him!! Wouldn't that be nice? Close now and please write soon! How much longer are you going to stay, Honey? Here are all my love and kisses.

XXXXXXXXXXXXXXXXXXXXXXXXXXXXXXXXX

Your darling wife,

Rose

I did not know my father in his life with Rose, but I glimpse him in these letters, I see him in the home movies he made of my brother Jack and sister Joan at Christmas; how free he was in displaying his love for them. I see him in the madcap train robbery video he made with Rose's brothers. I see him dressed up as a vaquero in a Halloween costume party with Rose's friends and family. I see the baby book she kept so lovingly of my brother Jack when he was born in 1928. I see her smiling, dressed up as a gypsy at a costume party a few years later. I feel Rose through a lifelong sense of loss and longing that my older sister Joan felt, after losing her mother at such a young age. The meaning of Rose in the lives of my older brother and sister gave to them their creative drives. The loss, and Rose's strong spirit of love, endorsed in them a very deep bond between brother and sister throughout their lives. They were like twins. Yes, that close. And they were the central pillars in the lives of my siblings and me. (Jack and Joan died only three days apart. Joan of complications from a stroke; Jack from cancer.)

Rose died at the age of twenty-seven after complications from a surgery for excessive uterine bleeding, leaving her two young children rudderless. Two years later Leong Shee felt that it was time for San Tong to return to China to get hitched again.

My mother, Yee Lai Ping, was nineteen years old when she married my father who was thirty-two years old. She and her family lived in the Town of Sun Wui, which is a one-hour drive north by car from Sum Gong Village and which is in the Pearl River delta of Guangdong Province.

Leong Shee contacted her girlfriend in "Five Villages," which is a cluster of sub-villages located at a bend in the Tan River northwest of Leong Shee's birthplace of Ma Choong Village. And Ma Choong, mind you, is a hamlet located fifteen-minutes north of Sum Gong Village as I've said to you earlier.

"Will you be my son's matchmaker?" queried Leong Shee to her longtime childhood friend in Five Villages.

"Of course!" banged her friend's craw, who continued with excitement, "...and this is how we do it...you bring your son to...." Blah blah blah, she chuckled onward as if the years and the oceans had never forced the two friends apart.

The matchmaker was also a friend of Ping's teacher, and so, these two women arranged with Ping's mother Madam Yee the following: Ping would deliver "wedding cakes" to the teacher's home to announce her sister Fay's impending marriage; wedding cakes are like "Save the Date" reminders in Chinese custom.

Ping was caught by surprise: at her teacher's home, San Tong and Leong Shee rose from their chairs to greet her.

But I pause a moment to share with you Ping's *jiapu* (family tree), which the matchmaker, the teacher, and Madam Yee had checked to conclusion before the arranged meeting.

Ping's father, Yee Ngan Ban, was Governor of Hainan Island in the last years of the Qing Dynasty. His appointment was hard fought. For the first time since the Manchu had come to power, and after prolonged social unrest in China, the Manchu Emperor allowed Chinese to serve in government; however, only if a Chinaman could pass the Palace Exams. This meant passing at the Municipal Level, then the Prefect Level, then advancing to the Provincial Level, and finally, to the Palace Exams held on Palace grounds. At the palace grounds, you were locked inside a cubicle for three days and nights answering question about Confucian whatnots. If successful, you were assigned a rank. If you ranked Number One, you were appointed to a position in the royal palace. If you ranked Number Two, you were appointed as the governor of a Chinese province. In Yee Ngan Ban's ranking, he was appointed Governor of Hainan Island, and as Governor, you had to hire your own military and develop commercial enterprises to support your administration. Therefore, these enterprises were quasi-government owned. Moreover, Hainan Island is situated between Southern China and the Gulf of Tonkin. So, the Island served as a strategic military outpost for the Chinese empire: it had a close view of Vietnam to the west, and a sweeping view of the South China Sea on which the Paracel Islands and Spratly Islands bobbed into view.

Ping's oldest brother Ah Yook died in Hong Kong. He was survived by her older sister Fay, followed by Ping herself, and finally, Ping's youngest brother Ah Jao whose twin sister had died in infancy.

On October 10, 1911, the Wuchang Rebellion in Wuhan, Hebei Province, led to the fall of the Qing Dynasty and the rise of Sun Yat-sen.

Under Sun Yat-sen's new Republic of China, Governor Yee Ngan Ban was appointed District Circuit Judge in which he travelled throughout Sun Wui District presiding over legal disputes; everyone had scores to settle in the days after the fall of the Qing Dynasty. Governor Yee came from a family whose members were by tradition attorneys and judges, and so, the job suited him fine. But during the Red Canton Uprising of 1927, in which communists led by Mao Tze-tung and nationalists led by General Chiang Kai-shek clashed, Governor Yee Ngan Ban died. Ping was only nine years old at the time.

That was then, this is now.

The Town of Sun Wui, located one hour north of Sum Gong Village, buzzed with excitement. Word tore round Town about San Tong Jue and Yee Lai Ping's pending marriage. San Tong's cousin Mansui would serve as the "matron auntie" to oversee the wedding. This was Chinese custom. And at sixteen years old, Cousin Mansui was thrilled to be part of the action. Mansui was the daughter of Jue Joe's younger brother Jue Shee; yes, that Jue Shee who let fly his Tommy gun at San Tong in a fit of squabble with Leong Shee decades earlier!

To Mansui, the man who came to see her had a serious bearing: he was tall like a storybook lord. He was swathed in an ivory suit, matching Panama hat, and white suede shoes. In other words, he was a Gold Mountain man. Mansui saw that her cousin San Tong perspired not from the heat of the Delta's summer, but from that awkward toe-tripping kind. At the age of thirty-two, San Tong appeared in her midst smelling of Victor's pomade shellacking his hair smooth, and he talked of dowry. He'd brought to Mansui her purpose that day—the role of matron auntie—and she gave a chuckle at life's simple pleasures. Although China's war with Japan loomed ever closer to Jue Joe's extended family, mirth was the moment's action for this congress. For no one in Sum Gong Village and in Sun Wui Town wished to miss San Tong's wedding day. To folks of the Pearl River delta, a wedding was a needed boost inside geography gone so mean.

Nineteen-year-old Ping's innocence would soon feel China's worry, but for now, Mansui felt her surrogate calling to protect this occasion. For Sun Wui was the birthplace of her husband-to-be, the palms merchant whom the Red Army would pancake later. Now, as the "matron auntie," Mansui knew she had to work with speed because, in the wake of Japanese bombings, and the Red Army's advance into the Pearl River delta, and the White Army of the Nationalists in hot pursuit of the Red Army, her breath rotated faster than she could swallow. She made the bridal couple bow three times to ancestors gazing down from their portraits, and then she--

"Blockade!" interrupted a runner in panic, he'd burst upon the ongoing ceremony looking white as a caged bunny. He threw a gong-cry, "The Japanese have taken Jiangmen Harbor!"

Mansui knew that Jiangmen Harbor, which was an hour's ride north by jitney, was the only way to and from the Pearl River delta.

"The Dollar Steamship Company has docked its *President Hoover Line* in Jiangmen Harbor," continued the runner, "it's gonna run the blockade!"

Mansui's voice broke with urgency at San Tong, "No one sinks a Yankee clipper, Cousin, you and Ping must go! The *President Hoover Line* is your only hope!"

The *President Hoover* in a devil maneuver rammed through the Japanese blockade. It won freedom for San Tong and Ping, though it was torpedoed and sunk on its following run of the Japanese blockade.

Below deck San Tong told Ping that they would finish their wedding vows in Hong Kong before a justice of the peace, as in the American way.

But a kid kept bawling, Jack. He was San Tong's little cousin in Sum Gong Village. Little Moe was to be the "paper son" of San Tong's late brother, San You, who died of leukemia in Los Angeles without a son as his heir. And Little Moe was to sail to California with San Tong and Ping on the *SS President Hoover.* Jue Joe had purchased the "birth certificate" for Moe in Los Angeles' Chinatown, which described a healthy boy eight years of age living in China. Poor, poor little Moe. He was four years old and was floating toward the morgue. For Moe was a sickly lad with a wok-belly and a runny nose. He was the son of San Tong's first cousin Ah Fook, who was in turn the son of Jue Joe's youngest brother Jue Yau who had never left the Jue compound in Sum Gong Village. Confusing? You bet. But this is how Chinese continue the bloodline of a branch in a family that has no male heirs; you adopt a son from another branch to be the "heir" for the branch having no son. And now, little Moe pelted his displeasure at abandonment of high adventure.

On the Jue Joe Ranch my mother Ping had a sideline. Writing. I remember her writing letters to her mother and to her teacher in China. This was her weekly ritual. Upstairs in the nursery room, she would sit at a desk and peruse a Chinese dictionary, then on paper squirrel calligraphy in vertical columns from right to left. War heaped terror on Madam Yee and the teacher, my mother told me. Daily bombings splayed buildings and people and there was no escape. So, my parents sent them money to ease their hardship. Soon, my parents sent them money to escape to Hong Kong; Madam Yee and her children stole into night in a sixteen-foot rowboat. Ping's teacher could not flee China. When my mother Ping had married in 1937 and sailed for America, she did not know that this would be the last year that she would ever see her mother.

China's Civil War intensified; daily, refugees pressed into Hong Kong. Madam Yee and her family crammed into a rat-infested tenement in Mongkok in Kowloon District, Hong Kong, in which disease mowed down tenants as quickly as newcomers arrived.

Madam Yee fell gravely ill with tuberculosis. Even so, my mother Ping wanted to see her mother. So, my parents arranged to take my sister Pingileen and me with them to Hong Kong. This is because Pingileen was five years old, and I was three years old, and we could travel for free.

It didn't happen. Before our departure, my parents learned that a U.S. law prevented my mother's reentry into the U.S. because she was not a Naturalized U.S. citizen and was also the spouse of San Tong Jue who was not a Naturalized citizen either.

Three months later my mother received a letter from her brother Ah Jao in Hong Kong. Their mother Madam Yee was dead. Ping was devastated. I saw her weep every day for all that could have been and was not. One day, our Adohr milkman who delivered milk to us found my mom crying. She told him why. The white-uniformed milkman turned to me and said, "You be a good little girl, now, take care of your mother. She needs you."

Hong Kong has another story to tell, Jack. In 1937 Jue Joe had instructed San Tong to find suitable land in Hong Kong on which to relocate the "Jue Joe Family" in California. It was always Jue Joe's desire to move his family and himself back to China, especially when anti-Asian sentiment in America ripped full throttle across its character. But San Tong rejected the idea because China was at war with Japan, and Jack and Joan were born in Los Angeles and were attending school there. He wanted them to have an American education and to have a better life that was best realized in America.

As history would unfold: Japan occupied Hong Kong from 1941 to 1944.

"Pa wanted me to be the farmer because I'm a quiet sort," explained Father, after I'd asked him to elaborate. "He wanted my brother to be the marketman at the Produce Exchange because he was the oldest. After the death of San You in 1933, and after the death of my first wife Rosemary two years later, the Depression hit us hard. If we were to sell the Jue Joe Ranch and sail to China as Pa had wanted, we'd have gotten only $12,000 for the whole of it. For all the years that Pa had toiled, first as a migrant performing stooped-labor, then as a farmer and marketman who struggled to invest in the American dream despite Exclusion Laws against Chinese—this was too much for him to bear. Everything Pa had lived for, everything he strived for, had slipped through his fingers and he was so unhappy.

"The night Pa passed from us he was sweating so badly. I remember a lit hurricane lamp by his bedside that showed me his torture. Beads of sweat ravaged Pa's face and body; it soaked his bed clean through. But it notified me that Pa was alert and still had a mind sharp as a razor because he knew his ulcer had burst, though he wouldn't let me take him to a hospital.

"He pumped at me a hard whisper, 'Son, they plays with you by flash'in saws. I told you this so many times!'

"In my attempt to comfort Pa, I said to him, 'You'll pull through this o.k., don't you worry.' Pa went ballistic, he yelled at me, 'A FOOL can see I'm a goner.' But behind Pa's tough exterior I saw that he was heartbroken for all that he couldn't give to his family. The Depression had cut him down hard.

"And before dawn on February 26, 1941, that agony was what Pa carried to his grave.

"After Pa died, I was determined to make good for us. And believe me, it was scary. We were in debt up to our ears. No matter what happened at the Produce Exchange, or in the fields on our farm, I had to clear at least ten-thousand dollars a year just to make ends meet. I *had* to do that."

San Tong Jue shouldered that burden for the rest of his life.

CHAPTER 7 – RANCH TIMES

I am six-years old and perched on top a trash can. My throne smiles by a fireplace in our living room in Father's new house on the Jue Joe Ranch. What a magnificent manor I can see: our house is two stories high and is 3,817 square feet. It's a far cry from the 20 x 40-foot, Redwood cottage that I'd spent my one- and-a-half years crawling around. In that cottage, I remember asparagus shoots exploding through its floorboards. Two termite holes took me each time I crawled toward the front door, too. But a big hornet's nest that hung in front of the old cottage's kitchen window—the one that always had to be kept shut—well, it was a trip to hear those flying beasts knocking against our windowpane.

In the home built by Father in 1945, a rose-colored silk carpet presses a hush over our large living room. The silk carpet complimented a formal dining room dressed in elegant Chinese décor. I remember being told not to run wild near my Grandmother Leong Shee's bedroom, which was situated by a busy front door. "You must respect Grandma's need for quiet," reminded my father's voice. "She's not in good health. She's toiled so hard all her life and can now enjoy some luxury. Use the kitchen's side door to play outside."

Follow me to an indoor atrium and you will hear canaries chirping; they splash and bathe from tiny porcelain bowls attached to their cage. The atrium's sweet scent explodes from tropical foliage that Father had potted round the atrium: Birds-of-Paradise blooming with mango-red flowers, soft green ferns, pink whisks of florals, and broad-leafed palm plants. This morning I sprayed a canary's feathers with DDT to clean its quills. No, no, not a good move. The congress dressed me down.

From our atrium a narrow hallway steers you toward a den, a bathroom, my Aunt Dororthy's bedroom, and, of course, Leong Shee's private repose by the front door; her bedroom is next to the wide front door in case an ambulance must call. A silver-framed mirror commands this hallway, too. Beneath the mirror is a built-in counter on which sits a black box with a mouthpiece, and it has a rotary dial. Underneath this counter are slots for Jack and Joan's collection of *Okeh* records. But projecting from our den is a standup radio console powering action: President Harry S. Truman's voice breaks aloud, "Inchon...today we took...God bless our brave young men...God bless America...." So, I polish a Chinese character carved into our white front door. It is a character called "Fook" (or "Fu" in Mandarin), which means "good fortune." We are favored safe passage through wars and whatnots with this blessing. At the request of

Father, Leong Shee had chosen this word to bless our new home. But Harry S. Truman continues, "…help our troops, our nation, by buying American war bonds!"

Draftees? We get'em on our ranch like birds alighting on an old plantation. The arithmetic is simple, you needn't bomb the Yalu River in Korea if you're foraging on a farm for Uncle Sam, keeping boxcars rolling for boys who need C-rations while they fight for our freedom on the Frontline.

One day, Father explained himself to me after a long day of hard work in the asparagus fields. He said, "About Grandma, I built this new house for her because she's lived a rough life, you know. I want her to see that I'm doing well and that she need not ever work again. She can enjoy my success." He was proud of how he'd brought our family out of hard times.

San Tong worked the Jue Joe Ranch in Van Nuys—which he renamed to honor his father after the latter's death in 1941—he worked the Ranch from sunrise until sundown. Then, each morning, San Tong drove at 3 a.m. to the wholesale Produce Exchange on San Pedro Street, in Downtown Los Angeles, to market fresh crates of asparagus nationwide; each crate stamped with our logo of "Universal No. 1." He worked round the clock to build a dream.

How I love the house that Father had built in 1945. Its rooftop gives me a sweeping view of the San Fernando Valley: farms as far as you can see, a few stores set here and there, and come evening, the sound of coyotes bending through the Valley. Our two-story manor has sideboards painted toothpaste white and has windows flanked by brick-red shutters. And make no mistake. The Jue Joe Ranch is, like the Valley's character, self-sufficient as an economic unit. Across the Ranch's green fields on which hand-plows have scratched their signatures, you see a gasoline pump, a tool shed, horses' stables, redwood barns, and there, there standing next to Vanowen Street, you see Jue Joe's pumphouse with an artesian well inside. Father keeps the pumphouse padlocked so that we kids will not enter and vanish as an echo. We have the usual hens socking out eggs, too. Between Jue Joe's cabin and the edge of our asparagus field, a large chicken coop commands attention. It is filled with carrier pigeons. These World War II flying relics were released at the end of the War only to find themselves sharing life with hens in that coop on the Jue Joe Ranch. The pigeons find themselves turned into squab once a week for our large, extended family. But an old rooster in that coop gives protest day and night for our impudence.

On the Jue Joe Ranch there are trees bearing ripe apples, oranges, lemons, nectarines, plums, and walnuts to satisfy your palette. There are apricots, figs, peaches, dates, grapes, and honeysuckle that in their twain perfume the air round the Ranch when you pace its metes and bounds. Healthy vines corkscrew up bamboo sticks and hang their fruit for you to harvest. Come with me to the backyard and you'll find a figure-eight shaped swimming pool beckon you to float across its turquoise surface. You will see an open bathhouse by that pool, too, and it has showers and lockers and a barbecue pit, which means a picnic table and benches and our family enjoying the Valley's rustic moods. Here sits Leong Shee's black-iron stove, too, heaving with character centuries old; it is a reminder of where we've been and where we're going. Clearly, Father has brought to our large, extended family a vision of an immigrant's dream come true.

One day my father motioned me off my trash can by the fireplace. He said to me softly, "Come over here and see your Grandma." My eyes drank in a tiny ancient swallowed by a couch. In the living room I could see that the pain of living—her's—hit Father hard and he's spelling out those bruises to me. He's trying to make me understand an immigrant's story. But Grandma seems too old to have lived those tales of a young woman in an old country raising her two sons all by herself.

In that room Father lights up a Lucky Strike cigarette. He draws a few puffs and points me to a portrait hanging above the hearth's white mantel. My eyes lock onto the sharpness of Jue Joe's perries piercing down and into my soul. For the photograph of this man looms with large impact upon the congress of us all. He is there, always there in hover above our hearth, boring into the heartbeat of our congress.

"This is our family's headquarters now," says Father to me. He taps Jue Joe's portrait above the fireplace and says, "Our new home should have a bit of the old country built into its spirit. I want the Jue Joe Ranch to be the central beacon in all our lives, a home to which you can return whenever you wish. It's like a ship anchored safely in a harbor that will always provide for you—that will always provide for everyone in the family—because it is our only headquarters now. We can't go back to China."

As a ten-year-old I hear my father's mental gears shift. "What is Sum Gong like? you ask me. Well, life is simple. You live close to earth, feel for the direction in which a monsoon blows, then you open rice fields to plenty of water for things to grow." He is lost in thought, then continues, "I can remember riding with my friend on his family's water buffalo down a rice field and I was struck by how beautiful a simple sunset is, all golden hues, then a deep red, it's a stunning image that still lives with me."

There is a life hidden in Father's interior that I want to know. I rummage through his books placed carefully in a built-in bookcase set behind his wing-backed chair, the one by the fireplace in our living room. I traverse the far reaches of the globe through a sampling of his books. A set of volumes from our past revisits me: a few of Jue Shee's handbooks on science and mining that had refused to sail with him to Harbin, China, years ago when he'd sold Jue Joe's business and skipped the country. Now, those leather-bound, worn jackets stare at me entwined with a dream unrealized in America. But Father's volumes of the Encyclopedia Britannica that command the shelves of the bookcase, well, these volumes speak to me of knowledge that's possible to realize. And I do love words: happy words, sad words, angry words, words of comfort and words of warning. I listen to words about the history of our clan, too, of which I am the runt living under our roof on the Jue Joe Ranch. There is my Grandmother Leong Shee, my parents San Tong and Ping, my brothers Jack and Guy, my sisters Joan, Soo-Jan, and Pingileen; and there are my aunties Corrine and Dorothy, and my Cousin Chan Lum Loon (alias, Sik Loon on his immigration papers). Their chorus of words form idea in me. There's a shadow-play bouncing into view: I begin to understand what my father speaks of with great emphasis to us all—what the word "family" means in an immigrant's conclave.

For I see heirlooms asleep in the house that have journeyed far to reach our younger generations on the Jue Joe Ranch. Now, they lay about as useless objects rusting with their long-forgotten memories. They are small reminders of an ancient link that refuses to skip from mind and that demands a corner of our souls: Leong Shee's Ming trees and wooden idols and scissors with huge loops for handles that she used to make one new garment once a year for her two sons in Sum Gong Village. I see her tins filled with dried tangerine peels and red dates. I smell her medicinal poultice that unearth one's faith in village ways. And always, I feel the ancient ways of Old China when I see her chart of bodily meridians that hawk of where to twist little pins for healing.

Suddenly, I touch again the cypress trees—sharp as blades—that guard our kitchen's side door. Sweet-smelling aromas bounce from white gardenias to perfume our front porch. For days I've hosed the plants that skirt round our big house. And today, their blossoms explode across the acreage of our lives. And there, there in a cement pit built below our basement's window, which Father had designed to prevent the rain from entering, I hear the cry of new-born kittens.

Leong Shee brains a gopher teething on her carrot. She hates leachers in her garden. She pulled up the mauled root and her voice shook the world with rage. She was so upset over disrespect for her nurtured newborns. This is why Wino Mikey waits until she's out of sight, and when the coast is clear, he staggers back to her carrots. If you count stalks of carrots in her garden, you'd be minus ten in a day. For Mikey knows the way round Leong Shee's verdant garden. In one of our horse's stables, Wino Mikey flops each night, near those leafy carrot stalks. Father couldn't persuade him off the Jue Joe Ranch and so the old man waggles round the premises like a woozy stray. Sometimes I'm scared of that coughing relic because there's a world inside him that no one knows.   Nevertheless, Wino Mikey had joined our tribe of wandering strays.   I swear that Mikey never hurt me, but just the same, I keep clear of him depending on how his mood swings.

He worked for Father for one season in our packinghouse, and in the din of that barn filled with happy chatter of women grading asparagus on a conveyor belt, Mikey muttered at them incoherently.   He drooled too.   One day he staggered onto that women's assembly line and jammed asparagus tips sideways and down in field crates. Father discovered Mikey's handiwork too late: the green shoots were splayed to hell.

"Screw you!" flailed Mikey's maw at me one day.   I'd complimented him on his new hat.   It was olive-drab and could only have been lifted from the city dump.   But the chewed-up fedora lifted Mikey up a notch—what pumped from his interior, that is—it brought out a dignified old soul who'd seen life's upturns once and who'd proudly pinned on his fedora a worn-out medallion for remembrance.

Today, Mikey tips his fedora in greeting to me and I know he is o.k.   That is, until WWI spins the slabs of him squirrely again.   From the Salvation Army Mikey's pants have generous pockets, too.   He brings out a pint of gin from one pocket to show me. He tells me this flask is for, "—fenc'in my blues."   But I say to him, "Don't!   That's dynamite, Mikey."

"It does a soul good," offers Wino Mikey.   His unshaven cheeks split wide like a crab's.   Mikey must have lived through great events that I don't know about, so I color him purple, as if he'd been boiled alive in the human crock.   I draw my distance from Mikey accordingly: a flushed face means I should approach him with caution.   A red face means I should drop from his sight. On the Jue Joe Ranch it's one step forward with Mikey, and sometimes two steps backward. This is the measure of life with range folk.

What wondrous strays I've been honored to know on the Jue Joe Ranch. Too soon they vanish, twice a week for Mikey in the City's slammer. That's where I'm told he lives now; only, I know he'll come home, home to where his watermark stretches a clapboard on one side of the horses' stable, for it too acknowledges that this is Mikey's turf. More than once I saw him open his fly and hose that woodwork. I didn't take my eyes off that and he didn't catch me.

But the day that Mikey engraved his soul onto our hearts, well, he remains there with us forever. That morning Father showed me an article in *The Valley News and Greensheet,* a local newspaper that tallied with reverence the mood swings and whatnots of San Fernando Valley folk.

"A drunk was listed in a police report," dragged the rag-and-print words across my soul. "He was released last night from the City Jail. He walked into on-coming headlights of a pickup truck on Vanowen Street and—"

Mikey? But the distillery in his mind brought to him incoming rounds on a battlefield. Flashes he saw that night, I'm sure, but not from headlights on a pickup truck. This is because the medallion pinned to his fedora told me something that he was proud of. Courage. He had courage to take life however it came at you. He was trying to come home to our Ranch; the land he saw as his extended family. Suddenly, I felt beads of tears run down my face.

There is a truth about farm life. It is born of simple rhythms. It is honest in its complexities. I know this every day on the Jue Joe Ranch: the flies buzzing our barnyard as if surveying a tender concourse. Buckwagons and tractors bumping slowly down our asparagus fields; they work side by side to define what rows of crops should be born. On the ground a rubber tire lies abandoned amid weeds. Over there the butterflies shift in harmony as if to the strains of a lullaby. Here a broad gust of wind, there an old redwood barn tilts toward its weaker side. There's a hypnotic *whoosh* in the bushes, and this rural rhythm rustles your spirit as in Old China's eternal sonnets. The walnut trees, fig trees, apricot trees, the nectarine and orange and lemon trees stand tall against an approaching twilight. And rising full throttle over eucalyptus trees—the branches bent in salute to Vanowen Street—songbirds swing across their turquoise then onyx sky.

I have high regard for those who labor on a farm. Their postures bent over; their faces tanned by a burning sun. These silhouettes fill my horizon. They are sweating. Their boots are bought from a thrift shop. And those heavy boots move field crates from row to row and onto sleds driven by mules. Filled to overflowing, the sleds head for our packinghouse. In the distance of time, I see the last of our slow-moving mules, the strongest mare that Father had kept against the onslaught of tractors and harrows. The mule has been with us longer than I, and she knows to pull her asparagus sled filled with fresh harvest back to the right barn. The old mule knows every worker on the Jue Joe Ranch too.

"It's a backbreaking job," says Father as he catches me watching the farm workers. "It is ten to twelve hours a day—seven days a week—you stoop and rise until your back hurts; until your legs and shoulders and arms can't stand no more. But you can't stop neither—you gotta take those shoots just as they come up! You pick'em when they're seven- or eight-inches high. And they pop up day or night, and day or night you pick'em. Even when we think the day's over, they pop up come evening, and we gotta be out there with lamps lit and we gotta skin that field."

I pick up something heavy in our asparagus field. My tool is a two-foot-long, medieval weapon. It is forged of iron and its tip is forked like a rattler's tongue. Father shows me how to uproot expertly the earth's green quills with this machete. Like a reaper of old Song Dynasty times, he thrusts his machete at a steep angle—as if brushing the face of an exquisite scroll. Soon, I follow my father's motions, feeling clumsy with my iron rattler until, finally, I can do it, reaping asparagus shoots until the ground sings with the echo of a timeless rhythm.

Father is steeped in this life, I tell myself. Verbena flows across his personal acreage. I see the field's stardust settle like silken specks on his hair and it softens the monkey grease routing across his suntanned face. I see dirt buried beneath his fingernails, and when I kiss his rosy cheek, I taste the salt of the South China Sea. Father subtracted from his life the briefcase drill-team adored by others in the New World. He didn't graduate from the halls of ivy, but finally, when the San Fernando Valley acknowledged the contribution of its pioneers, he was invited to teach students at Pierce College, in Woodland Hills. It was on a weekly basis. He passed to his students knowledge of the loam's mysterious treasures, and those students learned the moods of the San Fernando Valley's temper. They learned to follow its permutations and to polish and powder its natural face. They learned to test its alkaline membrane for the perfect moment to sow a seed. They learned to ride with Father on a harrow, churning its steel disks to pattern a field's new complexion. So, the hues brought on by wind and water took the students at Pierce College, and gave to each one, the magic to spread new life upon the lands of the San Fernando Valley.

The iron grasshopper that Father had crafted from parts rusting on the Jue Joe Ranch bolts him forward, then zig zags out of control. He'd built this tractor by hand, using a John Deere engine. He'd read issues of *Field Mechanic* and then customized the tractor's body to fit the narrow width of rows in our asparagus fields. Now, the greenhorn crashes into our packinghouse. And inside that packinghouse a one-foot-long, black panther bolts for the door. "Inky" is her name. We'd found her as a stray kitten and adopted her. And now, Inky's grown but still thinks in blades of, well, panther logic. Meaning here a nose, over there a feather of a what-not, dropped at our front door.

Outside the wounded packinghouse, Inky brings a thing into shock-bright sunlight. It swings between her fangs. She drops her newborn baby into Father's concrete irrigation bowl nestled in the asparagus fields; it's one of many designed by Father and spaced at intervals down each row. Inky returns to drop another newborn in another bowl, repeating this until she feels assured that all six of her kittens are safe from harm.

In frantic dismay, my siblings and I follow high-pitched *meows* that lead us to Father's irrigation bowls. We pluck each kitten up and place it into a cardboard box; its fate spared from a gush of water into the bowl to sprout new growth in the asparagus fields.

The hens take issue with me, too. In our chicken coop, a flock of hens strike at me with bladed boots. With quickness I drop their eggs from my apron. But carrier pigeons in the coop show me a peculiar move: in midair they pirouette up the sky only to bang their heads against a chicken-wire ceiling; their bodies bumping down nests of wooden cubbyholes that take the backside of the coop from floor to ceiling. Their stunned beaks give it up. Their squirrely sounds hit the ground. For in the coop, I catch a figure bouncing from one foot to the other. My Cousin Loon is working this space too. In his hand he's opening a gunnysack.

I follow Cousin Loon who carts his sack filled with pigeons kicking, I follow him to a heavily shaded walnut tree. There, steam furls from a cauldron steeping, and the smell of wet feathers snares my curiosity. Cousin Loon explains to me how he prepares a village delicacy. His broad smile throws me slopes and angles of Sum Gong Village, its rivers coursing through the nervous fabric of our lives. Cousin Loon brings to us a gentle presence, a balance from chaotic emotions that power an immigrant's struggle to build a dream on the Jue Joe Ranch.

Jue Joe had sent for his grandnephew Chan Lum Loon some years earlier. Chan Lum Loon's grandfather Jue Nui had died in Alaska. This was later followed by the death of Chan Lum's father Shia Jeong (*alias,* Jew Man Jew) in Sum Gong Village; and

Shia Jeong was also San Tong's "first cousin" as well. Thereafter, Leong Shee looked after Chan Lum. So, Jue Joe had sent Chan Lum Loon a steamer ticket bound for Los Angeles, California, to be his personal driver around town and to learn the business of farming in America.

The way Jue Joe had put it to my father's ear, "...else he'll go haywire! I need to guide him." He always thought in terms of family, as dictated by Chinese custom. You look after one another. You move together as one entity. And this is how our tribe expanded across the western lands.

Today, Cousin Loon lives in Leong Shee's old cottage on the Jue Joe Ranch. As daylight drops low on the horizon, Cousin Loon stirs his cauldron under the walnut tree lodged between our packinghouse and our outhouse, which is used by workers on the Ranch.

"Whatcha gonna do?" I ask Cousin Loon. Terror knocks about in his gunnysack.

"Watch me closely," throws his throttle, yanking a pigeon from his sack.

Then, gripping his pigeon by its throat he sinks two thumbs into it. One sharp twist of its neck and its beak falls open. Its eyes roll backward. Feathers vanish into steam corkscrewing up from the cauldron. Poor poor bird. My fingers stroke the head of the next victim flailing between Cousin Loon's thumbs; the softness of its feathers touches my soul. Then a whiff of broth perfumes my nostrils as I watch the pigeon's innocence melt into the vastness of life's boiling pool.

As the day's shadow grows older, as I feel its dark wings widen across my world, I turn into our packinghouse with our black mutt named "Bingo." Bingo, as I've told you earlier, had come to us from Ortega's bar located on DeCelis Place—a dirt wagon trail—in which bingo games are often enjoyed by braceros after their long, hard day's work. Shorty had won the puppy in one round, and Bingo grew into the best guard dog that we ever had.

The inside of our packinghouse is hot, fusty, rending with the rank of body sweat. Horseflies hum incessantly, encouraged by stumps of asparagus rotting on the cement floor. An amber glow filters through knotholes in the barn's sideboards and I feel as though I'm in a forest catching beams of dust floating and they're all lit up. I watch braceros labor over heavy crates laden with asparagus spears. They wear on their corded faces a sagacious countenance. I see young and old women on which grimy aprons heave with wear from monotonous routine. I hear the women's lips prattle in a tongue that I don't understand. But to me it sounds lyrical and poetic. Then I witness more men pile asparagus onto a rubber belt that moves down a track of steel rollers, rollers whipping across the length of our barn, rollers groaning a hard medley through our lives. And at the other end of this track, gloved hands of women sort and pack the asparagus into crates. Then, working a giant shearing blade to lop off uneven stems in those crates, Shorty commands that shearing blade.

This is what Bingo and I see on the Jue Joe Ranch: a community humming with storied lives that on its surface may appear simple, humble, but scratch below its surface and you feel the rich complexities of sunburned hardship. You hear the roar of feelings, too, embedded in lives working the earth to grow a dream.

Year after year at harvest time Shorty fills my seasons. The sound he makes at the shearing blade rocks our packinghouse because so many green quills await his leveling. As seasons steal past, Shorty's hair spins more frost on which I notice twilight reaching a permanence across his broad forehead. He's weighted by chunky features and by the depth of warm sentiment. His face is square, filled with the art of living, this I see. Below Shorty's coarse eyebrows a pool of thought shoots to a stranger what may appear as rough regard. But truth be this: Shorty is an angel, that's how I read him. He moves me to envision his migrant's world. For he has a shine for strays of all kinds and that includes Bingo and me.

One day on Vanowen Street a truck ran over my sister Joan's collie "Jay." My mother had warned me, "Don't let Jay out of the house—the milkman hates dogs." So, I was bad penny for weeks until Shorty approached our house cradling a puppy. As I've said to you earlier, "Bingo" was Shorty's prize in a numbers game held at Ortega's bar, and we'd lost Jay.

"He's yours," said Shorty to my siblings and me. "And Bingo loves jalapeno cheese." I reached out to pet Bingo, but he charged from Shorty's arms and into the vastness of our pasture where, amid horseflies buzzing, he rolled happily in horses' apples. Bingo showed us his familiarity with life on the range.

One morning Bingo charged at a man in snowy uniform, his arm swinging a basket in which bottles with cream floating up the necks had paper tabs for tops. Monday: I hear the milkman ask my mom for a tincture of iodine, the welts on his legs require urgent attention. Wednesday: the milkman begs my mom for more bandages, it's for his other leg, he says. Friday: the snowy uniform storms our driveway swinging a baseball bat, and yells, "Where's that piece of shit? I'm making mustard outta that piece of shit!"

I tell you that Bingo patrols our habitat like Fort Benning poised on fifth alert. With horse's apples crusting his bob-wired fur—we pet him only with our feet. He won't let you shampoo his hair, too. Bingo hates water. Harassed by flies gnawing his ears bloody, Bingo roams our packinghouse to bum jalapeno cheese from his old friend Shorty.

Poor, poor Shorty. His worn frame finally gave out. Shorty's widow by common law couldn't get the banker to pork over his savings; she'd stormed the bank with their six children, but her supplications did her no good, the manager merely gave a nod and showed the family to the front door. Feeling that she had a life unaccounted for, at least in the Anglo community, she called upon my father for help. He offered to speak to the bank's manager on her behalf.

"...and the law says she can't access Shorty's account if she can't show me proof of actual marriage," explained the manager to my father. *"Actual marriage,"* emphasized the manager again. He leaned forward on his Bauhaus chair and tossed at my father a half-smile befitting the manager's charcoal-gray suit. Then, his blue eyes scrolled down my father's dusty khakis and his lips tucked at the corners.

"But she's got six mouths to feed," implored my father. He continued in earnest, "The law said all us employers of braceros supposed to deduct ten percent from their wages and send to you folks to deposit in Rural Savings Account and you give back savings to braceros when they finish contract. We did our part. Look, she told me she'd brought her kids to you the other day and—"

"Kids could've been borrowed," interrupted the manager, brushing back a lock of hair. He looked for high ground, "been reading Shorty's file, I find that his citizenship is most unclear to me. Can you elaborate on this matter? Would you care to admit that Shorty was an illegal?"

"Shorty earned his money in this community, and he put it in your bank, and you let him do that," countered my father. "He paid his taxes and—"

"It's a free country and anyone can do that. But as I told her, and I'm telling you, Sir, the law requires that she show me proof of, well, they shot their foot don't you agree?" insisted the manager.

Legal rigamarole bent Father out of shape. The fray couldn't be resolved, and Shorty's family had to seek the Jesus house for charity. They lived in a car for a while, too. It was a moment not forgotten by me, what I saw behind that incident. It brought home a painful point: that folk who busy themselves about the worthiness of others are themselves the wayward laity, invoking legal technicalities to protect their wants, and doing so in such an exploitative way.

U.S. Marshals with paddy wagons arrive on the Jue Joe Ranch. Twelve officers alight to take up positions. In slow motion the raid on our packinghouse begins. Imagine sounds of billy sticks smashing through barn doors. Imagine tin badges flickering in beams of light. In synchronization, brown silhouettes abandon hand trolleys loaded with asparagus crates. They lam.

"Freeze!" squawks a bullhorn. Silhouettes tighten like a knot. With quickness they explode helter-skelter in all directions.

"Migra!" flutters a circus of tongues in the packinghouse. "Aiy! Migra!"

In the eyes of immigration authorities, brown folks are marked for redelivery home. What!? pumps my interior. "No, no, these are my friends!" pops my voice aloud. I see my friends hurl themselves through windows of the Redwood cloister and into the freedom of open fields. They shoot for Bull Creek. They tack here, zigzag there, at each crack of the bullhorn. In an instant I'm left with the memory of their terror and an emptied vista on the Jue Joe Ranch. I know these faces that grind themselves into irrigation ditches to hide, their eyes hanging for help in a world unable to reckon with encounters. This is a happening played on our Ranch, always at the start of harvest, and each season I witness the reruns.

The brown silhouettes board paddy wagons. I'm filled with feeling that I'll never see my friends again. In a few moments the paddy wagons roll out our yard and down the DeCelis wagon trail. Near the packinghouse, I hear a U.S. Marshal flood my father's ear. The Badge hands him a pink slip, and he says, "You'll be notified who to contact in

San Ysidro if you can prove a worker's legal status. So long, Mr. Jue, we'll see you again next harvest!" He dips his hat and takes leave.

But the U.S. Marshal hadn't collared the one man he would have if only he could have. Ramon Navarro. Ramon has been on the lam from him for three seasons. Father had squirreled him into hiding at the first warning from Bingo. And Ramon's hiding place is off to one corner of our family room in the big house. Ramon's toilet has a small window with a yellow blind drawn down, its crochet ring swinging in distress. From the toilet I hear Ramon weeping. Soused one day, someone had squealed on him, and the Badge been gaming for him since. Thin and lanky, Ramon emerges wrapped in sad refrains. For he'll never know peace in America, his fate will keep him on the lam. Nevertheless, he is a member of our extended family on the Jue Joe Ranch. And when Ramon is not using our privy, he's living with Connie Valenzuela in Jue Joe's original living quarter: three rooms lodged inside the big barn that faces Vanowen Street, built in year 1919.

Her iron skillet commands a portable grill. She rolls dough on top of a Masonite board, which is secured firmly between two field crates propped on their ends. In the barn's communal kitchenette, she pats the dough in midair until it's thin as a wafer, and a stray like me passing through the big barn can count on her fresh tortillas. There is nothing that can beat the taste and texture of Connie Valenzuela's tortillas. She makes the best. Aromas corkscrew off the grill, inviting others to join in producing the day's main meal before siesta on the Ranch. That's when I see Connie and Ramon's two little girls playing by the door: the oldest looks not more than three years old; the youngest not more than two years old. Connie tells me that their names are little "Connie" and "Irma," in descending order.

I tell you that a migrant's dream unveils oddly curious prisms: persuasive tipsy that feeds the soul and that permutates circumstance. Richie Valens (shortened from Valenzuela), who is Connie's son by a previous liaison, is going to turn her life around if one believes in miracles. And I do believe in miracles. For the Lord gave Ritchie a blessing—the gift of song.

On his guitar Richie strums the rich chapters of his life. And it began on a crate that Father had used for a beehive on the Jue Joe Ranch. Richie howled like a cougar, drumming on that piece of wood, which toppled the crate and got its residents madder than hell. Thousands of bees gunned the air like bombers closing in for pellet practice. Since the year 1919, three generations of bees in the hive shared life on the Jue Joe Ranch. And now, now they unleashed spiteful swords. But in alpha fashion, Ritchie hurled a rock to startle the queen bee. She stopped pumping whatnots inside her cocoon. This caused a sudden evacuation. No, no, you saw folks hightailing to avoid unstable bees. Folks ran from our packinghouse, the barns, the stables, the pastures, the tool shed, even Jue Joe's cabin and Leong Shee's old cottage. You saw Bingo fly from his doghouse, too, hurling head-on into our swimming pool. It was the only time that Bingo ever enjoyed a swim.

"Gonna lose the purse on this," moaned Father. He had to shut down the farming operation for three days while the bees debated their next move. I remember that my siblings and I were confined inside our house, too. And for me those captive three days saw us splayed on the carpet in our living room to watch our TV's screen flicker with snow. Then up popped an Indian chief's head on the screen. Suddenly, *Sagebrush Theater* strutted across that prism. Hanging sideways from a galloping steed—Hoot Gibson shot pell-mell at nogooders. But without warning, my brother Guy transformed that screen. He hooked expertly the TV's dial using his toe and you couldn't challenge such a feat. So, Flash Gordon rescued a blond from clay-men oozing out of walls in the millennium cave, while evil Ming made escape in a spaceship.

The bees finally have new lodging: a big asparagus crate that Father had gifted them. At once we got the green light from Father to explore the world again. High tailing up to the roof of our indoor atrium and onto its long flat surface, we began to roller skate. We dared one another to stop our wheels at the rooftop's edge.

Ritchie Valens cut another record. A gold hit and he began a tour of the nation's circuit. Ritchie appeared on Dick Clark's *American Bandstand,* and we were so proud of him. It made Connie smile through her tears of joy. One day she said to my brother Jack, "It is snowing back East. My little Ritchie, he no get sick—I knit him sweater." Connie Valenzuela was the proudest mom you ever saw.

For Ritchie's music brought alive the nuance of a rich culture. It is a melody of the spirit. It is sonorous history clear as the lunar light. When you grow up among pastorals you feel the ripples of such character. This is what Jesus revealed to me, not the one who rose on Easter morning, but the one who rose from our tool shed six days a week. Jesus pronounced as "Hasoose," always wore a Mountie's hat that complimented his olive complexion. In Jue Joe's tool shed, he created magical things of wonder. He worked an anvil and his high, so very high boots groaned and I knew he was busy working iron but never too busy to be the storyteller to us kids. He told us tales of his ancestors who were ancient Mayans and I saw in him a bird of paradise and heard in him a god rustling across a rainforest. Living creatures were drawn to Jesus, too, for his eyes lit up and his lips pursed and that's when you heard him sing in a high-pitched voice the following:

"Twee twee caboose caboose / twee twee Hasoose Hasoose...."

You knew to trust the love and serenity that Jesus had for all living creatures. Else why would wild coyotes search him out? One day a mother coyote brought to him her cub to raise. Next day she deposited another offspring at his doorstep. By midnight he was enveloped in moonlight howls. True. She sensed in Jesus something spiritual; saw in him a true artisan. In fact, we all did. For it was on full display at the end of each harvest season. Fiesta. How I loved the joy of fiesta on the Jue Joe Ranch and what Jesus gave to this venue.

I saw Jesus craft the most beautiful pinata—a dove of peace—for all the children whose parents worked on our farms in Porterville, Saugus, and Jue Joe Ranch in Van Nuys, California. At Fiesta time everyone came together as one family. Mariachi music filled the air. Dancing and laughter stole deep into the night, and the sheriffs on security duty on our Ranch enjoyed the best time with us all.

CHAPTER 8 - ASPARAGUS BEEF

"I've found the spot," announces Pingileen. Her eyes expose anticipation. "Come with me." I follow my sister who is two years older than me. In her right hand, Pingileen cradles a miniature music box. I see that it is an upright piano. She lifts the piano's lid, and a vintage tune turns through my moment.

"You like how I did this?" queries my sister. She retrieves a Buster Brown shoebox on the ground and lifts its lid for my review. Inside, a thing lay bloated sideways, just as we'd found it in our swimming pool. We'd fished that squirrel out of the pool. It had slipped off a rock at the pool's edge while taking a sip—slipped off the prized sedimentary concretion that Father had searched for and found in the Simi Valley Mountains. And now, the bushy varmint rests on face towels wreathed with sprigs of marigolds, pansies, and ferns of asparagus. Two pearls and a nose glisten in winter's light; they vanish in shadows as my sister closes the shoebox and as we bury the poor thing to rest forever by Jue Joe's cabin on the Ranch. A cross of twigs transforms the mound into soft feeling as a melodious tune from my sister's miniature piano rolls poetic. I hear a prayer pour from Pingileen's lips. I bow my head in respect for this once spirited, but now zipped, squirrel on the Jue Joe Ranch.

I learn of death in other ways as well. My mother clasps a Western Union tightly to her chest. It was sent to her by her younger brother Ah Jiao who lives in Mongkok, Hong Kong. My Uncle Jiao speaks of very old rites—the need to perform them. This is because Uncle Jiao said that their mother had died. I have heard my mother's tales of her childhood and of my grandmother Madam Yu in Hong Kong whom I have never met. In my imagination, this grand lady in Mongkok is made of exquisitely carved jade. Swathed in silk robes roaring with peonies the elegant empress beckons me to her throne. Her cabochon ring flashes me blinding prisms: shots of rare imperial jade, or "glass jade" as this gem is often called. Then I learn that the empress coughs ferociously and her hanky is stained crimson red. So, I see the empress press an index finger to her Crayola-red lips, and in terror, she flees the Pearl River delta at midnight, squirreled away on a sixteen-foot rowboat, as civil war breaks Neanderthal across the Chinese parcels.

The year 1947 zigzagged Hong Kong into despair. I never met the jade empress living in Mongkok, Hong Kong, and now my mother weeps for her.

In Los Angeles we'd gotten our passports. We'd been vaccinated against cholera, typhoid, and tetanus for our pilgrimage to the Orient. Only, we couldn't go. The League for Oriental Exclusion in America had lobbied for passage of The Immigration Act of 1924, which barred Chinese wives from entry or reentry to America if their husbands "were not" U.S. citizens. Meaning that if my mother Ping travelled to Hong Kong she could not return to America because my father was not allowed to become a Naturalized U.S. citizen.

So, my mother never had a chance to bid farewell to her mother in Hong Kong. My mother was only nineteen years old when she waved goodbye to Madam Yu in the year 1937. I put my face to my mother's cheek and tasted on her the salt of lost returns.

On the Jue Joe Ranch I pass summer days absorbing its soft rhythms. There are two posts in our backyard that Jack and Joan had attached a bedspring and mattress to, and the swing rocks you slowly into dream on the moves of a breeze and a bird's lullaby.

But one day my sister Pingileen opens with a secret. "Listen up, don't you leak this to a soul," propels her larynx.

"How can I? This thing can't talk. It's dead," pops my craw. We are performing last rites for another varmint found motionless on the Jue Joe Ranch.

"I know something real big," revs my sister's engine. "This morning in our living room...wait." Her miniature piano had halted its enchantment, and Pingileen rewinds it. A tune restarts and my sister's motor bends the canvas of that sound. "This is heavy stuff," she continues, "they got to shouting in the living room: Aunt Dorothy at Father and Father at Aunt Dorothy and Grandma sobbing. It was terrifying. I took cover behind our dining room's French doors. Adjusting the shutters, I seen it all! I couldn't stop trembling; I was so scared! Aunt Dorothy was talking real bad things, and Father was pleading with Uncle Warren to reason with his wife."

Uncle Warren is Aunt Dorothy's new husband. I'm thinking, he's soon to know a facet of her that he didn't know. She's as sensitive as a Sherman tank. The urgency in Pingileen's voice continues, "I couldn't stop trembling because, you know, it got so bad that Father grabbed a blade. He waved it in front of Aunt Dorothy and then he threw it at the fireplace. And you know something? Aunt Dorothy wasn't scared at all. She just sat on the sofa throwing Father her usual defiant taunts. She said to him, 'Good, now I'm going to make a pauper of you.' And Uncle Warren he was shocked and—"

"What was the fight about?" queried aloud my interior. "Tell me everything."

"The fight started because Aunt Dorothy wouldn't give Father back his Porterville Ranch in Tulare County; the one he bought with his own saving's for his retirement but had to put in Dorothy's name. I heard Father ask Dorothy for its return because he's a Naturalized U.S. citizen now and she wouldn't do it. So, Uncle Warren asked Aunt Dorothy, 'Sweetie, to whom does the Porterville Ranch belong to?' Aunt Dorothy replies, 'Why, it's San Tong's.' And Uncle Warren says, 'Then give it back to him, Sweetie." Gosh, she went ballistic. She shouted at him, 'Don't take me for one of your goddamned patients having a busted hernia! Who are you to tell me anything? This is my affair. You both go to hell!' Then Grandma tried to talk her daughter out of this stew, but it did no good. Dorothy yells at Grandma, "You don't tell me what to do."

The strength of grievances, how they fester and multiply. In the end they destroy. But what do you really gain? From my lowest rung in family hierarchy, I glimpse the damage: Dorothy landed Father on his back staring at his Maker, his paws wiggling in midair. That's murder one. But to what degree culture clash can explode I have yet to learn in life, for I haven't this part of our verse digested, no, no, not yet. Arguments between Father and Dorothy escalate. A confluence of mighty rivers crashes against each other. Something registers all over Dorothy's landscape that demands a remedy, this I see. Along with Father's Porterville Ranch, she says she's taking the Jue Joe Ranch in Van Nuys, too, because title to both properties are in her name. I know two-thirds of the Jue Joe Ranch in Van Nuys had been sold to Southwest Properties for subdivision. Now, Dorothy is declaring its remaining one-hundred acres and Father's Porterville Ranch in Tulare County—all ninety acres of it—as her own to punish him. In 1942, he had purchased the Porterville property from Scott Manlove. It was farmland that he and Jue Joe had once leased for asparagus farming. After Jue Joe's passing, the land came up for sale and Father was proud that he could afford to buy the Porterville property from his savings, although he could not hold title to it because the Exclusion Laws were still in effect. Dorothy knew she held power over him and the family by virtue of her birthright citizenship, and she used it to satisfy her revenge.

Our destiny is in free-fall. For sons of China know that a farm's operation is an integral part of a family tied to good earth since ancient times. It carries a meaning far beyond that of mere definition. As such, the good earth cannot be segregated without a family's heartbeat ceasing to exist. That's how Jue Joe had felt. And that's how Father translates the founding patriarch's concern to us, embedded as Father is in the ways of China.

"The yield we've grown on Lots 690 and 691," said Jue Joe to my father in the early years, "fills boxcars for Uncle Sam. Keep our asparagus farm growing, Son, and when my first-born grandson Jackie comes of age, Lot 690 is his to continue the family operations. Lot 691 goes to Corrine and Dorothy as their separate inheritance."

Indeed, Father works the farm as if its lore is embedded in not only us, but the YOU WHO ARE YET TO BE BORN. I know in my heart that its luster is the lyric of my soul. Running west from Hayvenhurst Avenue to Bull Creek, I see Father's emerald carpet flicker beneath a brilliant sun. This is because my brother Jack Sr. had told Father about asparagus seeds called "Universal No.1" from his school at U.C. Davis; the high-quality seeds were developed at the University's lab in which spears take only three years to mature for market, and not the usual five years. Father purchased the new asparagus seeds from U.C. Davis and increased our farm's yield threefold. But I tell you, Jack, the lot-line that continues westward from Bull Creek to Balboa Boulevard, well, rough feelings fester beneath the surface of Lot 691. This is Dorothy and Corrine's parcel.

"I've hated your father since I was seven years old, Jackie," tamped Aunt Dorothy's craw down the ears of my brother Jack Sr. "I still hate your father and I hate this family and the whole stinking matter."

"You can't mean what you're saying," responds my brother Jack.

"Oh? We'll see about that, Jackie. He's got no right to interfere with my personal life. He's not my father!" retorts Aunt Dorothy. Her bitterness builds, "Goddamnit, Jackie, I do what I want and that includes what I do at the office. I did the bookkeeping for him, I was in summer break from classes at USC. Ok, ok, so he paid me, but why shouldn't I write myself checks whenever I want to? Everything's in my name and I'm being used! He uses me to hold the lands, so I'm doing your father a favor. A favor! Doesn't he see that, Jackie? I've got him over a barrel, I can shut down this whole operation like that. He had better lay off me because I don't have to do him any favors!"

The ties that bind our family together are vanishing. Aunt Dorothy's overthrow of Jue Joe's order is coming to light on me. Can you kill without remorse the continuity that binds the generations of a family together? She is consciously doing so. For the immigrant struggles and sacrifices of father and son for family cut no antique verse for her; no treasure held in the heart. Instead, she wants to shroud herself in American ways that hark independence for an individual.

Only, what a way to do it, grieves my soul. I record for you the following exhibits:

Exhibit A. "Dorothy slapped me," gasps Grandma Leong Shee to my father. Her tears brim with a deeper ache. In the kitchen of our big house, she showed my father the bruised apple stamped across her cheek. Grandma had scolded Dorothy for spending nights with Dok Wong of whom Grandma had a tale to tell. Mind you, this happened before Uncle Warren entered Dorothy's life. "You talk to her, Son. YOU make your sister stop seeing that man. I'm only thinking of her future, you understand. I told her this and, and she slapped me so hard." She sobbed again.

So disregarded by her daughter, Grandma Leong Shee took the only option that she had. For a mother knows that a son's duty on the home-front is to cancel incoming threats. A good son must obey his elders and respect the norms of convention.

This was my father's lifelong burden.

"I'm taking up with Dorothy right now," asserts Father, examining his mother's red wound, which is a Rorschach that will live on her cheek for days. He touches her bruise; she winces in pain. In that instant, Grandma's interior wonders if she had gone too far. She switches gears.

"Don't be too hard on her, Son," backpedalled her entreaty. "Who will marry a girl who attacks her mother? I don't want gossip to—"

"She's got no right to hit you, Ma."

"Son, I don't want this incident to get around town. Who would marry her?"

Soul-tablets old as bronze pound deep in Father's interior. He feels obliged to broadcast gong-cries to his American-born sister. He doesn't figure that Dorothy would defect from these canons in such a smashing way. Instead, he delivers to her a sermon as steadfast as Moses belting the Ten Commandments to his tribe.

"...and someday you'll thank me for this Dorothy," assures Father. These words followed his closing argument that she must end her love affair with Dok Wong.

"Oh? We'll see about that!" stokes a bitter tide brewing in Dorothy's inner ocean. A sneer spreads from her lips pursed thin as a pencil's line. It hints at dark pathos to come. Of what, I do not know. But it stirs in me a December chill.

Exhibit B. Tuition at John Hopkins University plus room and board plus wads of cash for extras in her transfer to the East Coast from USC. That's what Dorothy demands from Father in exchange for an amputation of Dok Wong.

Exhibit C. Home from John Hopkins University on the East Coast, and Aunt Dorothy's been living with us for two years now. She completed a premed major in Biology. I remember that World War II in the Pacific had ended, but not for our congress on the Jue Joe Ranch. In secret, Dorothy had eloped with Warren Moe. But she never told our family. Two years she been living with us and never told us of her marriage.

When Warren Moe left for active duty in the Pacific War, Dorothy returned to the Jue Joe Ranch to live, all the while gloating that she would inflict upon Father a fierce surprise. For it was Warren who, at the end of the Pacific War, appeared on our doorstep to tell Father of the couple's marriage. Warren Moe was shocked that our family did not know about their marriage.

Exhibit D. I found Father's letter addressed to my Aunt Corrine who now lives in Hong Kong. She and her new husband Lansing Kwok had moved to Hong Kong so that Lansing could run his family's business called the "Wing On Department Store." The Wing On Department Store had been a very famous chain of large retail stores that first originated in Shanghai on the Bund.

In Father's letter to his sister Corrine dated January 26, 1950, his words flew straight from his heart to her. He told Corrine what had led to the family's current crisis. He told her the truth. And in his own handwriting it was a heart-wrenching story.

See Exhibit D below, Jack. This is what your Grandfather San Tong wrote to your Grandaunt Corrine who was living in Happy Valley with her husband Lansing Kwok. At the time, the Fung Fai Terraces was a hillside development situated on Hong Kong Island with residences for the very wealthy.

San Tong's letter is addressed to Corrine at the Terraces in the following:

(A copy of his handwritten letter and return receipt for the letter follows this transcription).

Dear Ah How (Corrine),

I am writing you again on the trouble we having with DJ (Dorothy). In my letter just few days ago I told you I have sent her the $20,000 plus 7% interest as of 1947 to date, making total sum of $23,593.34 as demanded by her. Now she send the check back making further claims by demanding that I have to pay the Bull Creek (property) money again which she has already drawn the money back when she went to China. She claim the money she drawn was the money due her from the Jew family. She further demand that I have to return to her the paper she wrote for me to sign and she signed it too in regard to the $20,000 settlement of the Jew Joe Partnership. Now I cannot understand why she wants it back for it was she who made it and signed it, and signed your name too. She phone up this morning unless I comply to all her demand by end of this month then I would have to go and see her Lawyer. She means to tell me she will start Lawsuit. She also make demand that I have to give her certain sum of money about 30 to 40 thousand now for gift tax. I took the matter up with Blodget (her lawyer). He say do not make any fuss about it for it will make thing difficult for everybody because it is difficult to untie or change the matter that was set up long ago.

Yesterday I went to the bank and bought a cashier check for $23,593.34 and mailed to her with return receipt to show that I have paid. The return card came back to me signed 'D. Moe' (meaning it was printed) not in her regular handwriting. She did the same thing on the previous check I mailed to her.

Now she has gotten $23,593.34 and demands repayment for Bull Creek and 30 to 40 thousand beside. There isn't that much money left I am afraid after paying the income tax, st. (street) improvements etc. and to meet her bandit demand too. This matter has upset our household this few days we hardly cook or can eat. It has upset

Mother dreadfully she cry today. She ask Loon to take her over to see Dorothy and her husband. I know and I told Mother it won't do any good for I have heard Warren said Mother can't do anything because nothing is in her name, right in Mother's face.

When Dorothy got married and had the party here in the house I gave her $1,000 as present from me and Ping and she kept the check all these years never have cashed it and never thank me. I was thinking right along she was mad and didn't want any of my money. But today she list that also as one of her demands that I must make good of that check plus interest all this time.

When Jackie got married Mother ask Dorothy to get her one gold piece, she wanted it as gift when she takes the tea from her grandson and his bride. Dorothy told Mother there isn't any such thing. She said she has never seen them. That made Mother sick worry over it. She hasn't gotten over this yet. She know Dorothy has got them all.

I know you are thousands miles away. I do not like to trouble you but this whole matter is very serious, getting bad to worse just about to blow up. My whole family hoping that you could be here to settle this affair. We know you have good sense of reasoning.

As I told you above I mailed the cashier check to Dorothy. Now I am waiting to see what her next move is. I told her the $1,000 her wedding gift I will see to it that she get it but without interest. The Bull Creek deal is in fact all paid.

Best regard to you all. Tell Lansing hello for me.

Your brother San

Dated July 26, 1950

PS. -- If I had continue letting her take store blank checks and let her write any amount she wants for herself and whenever she wants then of course there will not be all this troubles but any person has a head to think that cannot be done to run business safely. The principle is wrong. I put a stop to it that started the trouble.

Mother said the property on Balboa side is yours and Dorothy's.Hayvenhurst side is for Jackie and the farming interest is for me to maintain to support the family whoever is in need and to the best of my ability and of course that depends on how much I can do and how favorable nature and market condition is with me is a determining factor as to how successful I can live up to.   Now this is Father's and Mother's wish why does Dorothy want to fight over it what authority she is using when she hasn't any at all in the matter?

1-26-50

Dear Ah How

I am writing you again on the trouble we having with D.J. In my letter just few day ago I told you I have sent her the $20,000.00 plus 4% interest as of 1947 to date making total sum of 23,593.34 as demaned by her. Now she send the check back making further claims by demanding that I have to pay the Bull creek money again which she has allready drawn the money back when she went China. She claim the money she drawn was the money due her from the Jew family. She further demand this I have to return to her the paper she wrote for me to sign as she signed it too in regard to the $20,000 settlement of the Jew Joe Partnership. Now I can not understand why she wants back for it was she who made it and signed it and signed your name too. She phone up this morning unless I comply to all her deman by end of this month then I would have to go & see her Lawyer. She means to tell me she will start Law Suit. She also make demand that I have to give her certain sum of money about 30 & 40 thousand now for gift tax. I took the matter up with Blodget. He say do not make any fuss about it for it will make thing difficult for everybody because it is difficult to untie or change the matter that was set up long ago.

Yesterday I went to the Bank & bought a cashier check for 23,593.34 & mailed to her with return receipt to show that I have paid. The return card came back to me signed "D Moe" not in her regular handwriting. She did the same thing on the previous check I mailed to her.

Now she has gotten 23593.34 & demand repay for Bull creek and 30 to 40 thousand beside. There isn't that much money left I am afraid after paying the income tax, st. improvements etc & to meet her bandit deman

This matter has up set our house hold this few days. We hardly cook or can eat. It has up set mother dreadful she cry today. She ask Joone to take her over to see D.J. + her husband. I know & I told mother it won't do any good. for I have heard Warren said mother can't do anything because nothing is in her name, right into mothers face.

when D.J. got married & had the party here in the house I gave her $1000⁰⁰ as present from me + Ping and she kept the check all these years never have cashed it and never thank me. I was thinking right along she was mad & didn't want any of my money. But to-day she list that also as one of her demans that I must make good of that check plus interest all this time.

when Jackie got married mother ask D.J. to get her one gold piece. she wanted it as gift when she takes the tea from her grandson & his bride. D.J. told mother there isn't any such thing. She said she has never seen them. That made mother sick worry over it. She hasn't gotten over this yet. She knaw D.J. have got them all

I know you are thousands miles away, I do not like to trouble you but this hold matter is very serious. getting bad to worst just about to blow up my hold family hoping that you could be here to settle this affair. We know you have good sense of reasoning.

As I told you above I mailed the cashier check to D.J. Now I am waiting to see what her next move is. I told her the 1000⁰⁰ her wedding gift I will see to it that she get it but without interest. The Bull creek deal is infact all Pd.

Best regard to you all. tell Lansing Hello for me.

Your Brother
Sun

If I had continue letting her to take store Blank
clerks & let her write any amount she wants for herself & when
ever she wants them of course there will not be all this
troubles but any person has a head to think that can
not be done to run business safely the principle
is wrong, I put a stop to it that started the
trouble

mother said the property on Balboa side is
yours & Dorothy's Haymenhurst side is for Jackey
& the farming interest is for me to maintain
to support the family who ever is in need &
to the best of my ability & of course that depends
on how much I can do & how favorable nature
& market condition is with me is a determining
factor as to how successfull I can line up to.

over

now this is father's & mother's wish why
does D.J. wants to fight over it what authority
she has she is using when she hasn't any
at all in the matter

Form 3806-S (Rev. 3-49)

Receipt for Registered Article No. 10833   Postmaster per 2

Fee paid 55 cents. Class postage u   POSTMARK

Declared value _____ Surcharge paid, $ _____

Return Receipt fee _____ Spl. Del'y fee _____
Delivery restricted to addresses:

in person _____, or order _____ Fee paid _____
Accepting employee will place his initials in space
indicating restricted delivery. 6608 Van _____

NOTICE TO SENDER—Enter below name and address of addressee as an identification. Preserve and submit
this receipt in case of inquiry or application for indemnity.

Mrs. Lansing Kwok   14 Sung Tai Terrace
_____   _____
(Name of addressee)   (P. O. and State of address)

                             Hong Kong
                             China

Form 3806-S (Rev. 11-48)   11052   Postmaster per 2

Receipt for Registered Article No. _____   POSTMARK

Fee paid 15 cents. Class postage au

Declared value _____ Surcharge paid, $ _____

Return Receipt fee _____ Spl. Del'y fee _____
Delivery restricted to addresses:

in person _____, or order _____ Fee paid _____
Accepting employee will place his initials in space
indicating restricted delivery. 6608 Van _____

1950

NOTICE TO SENDER—Enter below name and address of addressee as an identification. Preserve and submit
this receipt in case of inquiry or application for indemnity.

Mrs. Lansing Kwok   14 Sung Tai Terrace
_____   _____
(Name of addressee)   (P. O. and State of address)
                             China

Sad refrain in Father's words draw for me the irony of our odyssey. It is a tribe condemned to an ebb of fractured harmony. In this lair in which no one is free of this cultural parable, our family's truth is embedded in the earth it brings to life: some folk view the earth as communal; others view that same premium as divisible. Overnight, Dorothy deposits centuries of earth into her bank account for her separate token of freedom.

Regarding Dorothy's lawsuit, my father told me the following:

"I went to Dorothy before the courtroom trial began and I begged her, 'You can have whatever you want, but just leave me a small patch of land, just leave me enough to farm so that I can feed my children and care for our mother. Don't destroy our whole family so completely.' But she showed me only her contempt for all the hardship that our parents had endured to attain this much, and for my attempt to carry on in their wake.

"So, I thought that Corrine would stand by me. I needed her active support in this matter, and I wrote to her in Hong Kong. I trusted her, you see, and believed that she would reason with Dorothy. But her husband Lansing told her not to get involved and she didn't come to my aid."

It was then that I truly understood what was happening. I folded Father's letter and hid it in the back of Father's desk, the one in his upstairs office in our big house spinning with pain.

Mr. Blodget, Aunt Dorothy's attorney who'd been Jue Joe's attorney in the year of 1919, had put Lots 690 and 691 in a Trust for Corrine until she came of age. He used Otto F. Brant's Land Title and Insurance Company as Trustee, with Brant as beneficiary who would assign to Corrine upon her written demand. And when your father Jack Sr. who was Jue Joe's first-born grandson came of age, Aunt Corrine was to deed Lot 690 to him, as was Jue Joe's oral intent. When Corrine married and moved to Hong Kong, she assigned her interest to Dorothy, which gave Dorothy a windfall: the Jue Joe Ranch and my father's Porterville Ranch.

Attorney Blodget, fearing scandal that he had circumvented and manipulated Federal law and California's legal system because no Chinaman could legally own land, well, disbarment didn't look pretty to Blodget. He was easy picking for Dorothy. She knew that he had to back her because America's legal system turned on instruments of paper. She was certain that inheritance based on cultural traditions orally passed down were, in America, tossed in air as useless vapor.

So, the holder of legal instruments—the hand-printed "D. Moe"—assured Aunt May who was my Uncle San You's widow and who was disowned by Jue Joe following a beef with him, D. Moe assured Aunt May that she would get her share of the pie if she became a co-plaintiff with D. Moe. But after Dorothy's victory over my father, and in a separate contest that followed with Aunt May, Dorothy pinched her sister-in-law's share from her. Dorothy took control over the entire Jue estate. And control was her thing on many levels of her life, in my opinion. I had come to understand this peculiar trait that dominated her relationships with others.

Sad, I mean when you lose your fireside chats, when you lose your good earth on which you've culled a lifetime of dreams and on which you've created continuity for the generations. In this case, over one-hundred years of Jue Joe Ranch's history. The final truth is that you've lost your family. You've lost what a family really means, that is. And in final tally, you've lost a whole lot of yourself, haven't you? Right then, alone in the roar and rush of these feelings—I could feel my father's enormous heartbreak as never before revealed to me with such fullness.

CHAPTER 9 - HARVEST OF SORROW

I am seated in a courtroom. My father's fate will be decided here. My brother Guy slides into my pew, and panting breathless, he whispers in my ear, "...almost didn't make it. I told Father we'll be late to court; we can't stop along the way. I'm busting us down the freeway fast as I can, but he says to me, 'Stop here.' What can I do? I pull our car into the driveway of Rosedale cemetery, and we—"

"That boneyard?" I hear my throttle pump, as I catch Judge Palmer's glare aimed my way.

"Yeah, the one located on Normandy and Washington. I pull into Rosedale. Father jumps out of our car and walks to Grandpa Jue Joe's grave. He stands there with his head bowed and he, he talks to Grandpa."

"You do this often with him?" fires my engine. "You see him talk to Grandpa?"

"Every morning since this trial began," confirms my brother. He pumps more into my ear. "Every morning Father reports the court's proceedings to Grandpa. I pray we make it to court on time. Oh, how I pray!"

My eyes fix on Aunt Dorothy who doesn't notice me because she's directing her hired guns: Mr. Blodget, Mr. Copp, and Mr. Waring. Three aging cronies who are quoting all kinds of legal mumbo in the courtroom. I see that Aunt Dorothy is donned in battleship gray; her knit dress outlining her thirty-five years of confidence. Her dark hair is swept backward into a Josephine knot, and there's a little white bow clipped to that bun. The image is of a delicate female in distress. It's the charm offensive.

Poor poor Father. He understands that he is alone in this combat. The old-timers in Los Angeles' Chinatown who had known Jue Joe and who were scheduled to testify in court for Father regarding Jue Joe's *intent,* well, Dorothy rang each one up on the phone. To each old-timer she whipped, "You testify in court, and you'll be rowing down the Yangtze River, I'll have you deported! And I'll see to that myself!" This is what the old ones, weeping, told Father. She had the goods on them, they wailed. Many of them had come through immigration as "paper sons" with false identities and were deathly afraid of being found out. Above all, they feared deportation and the knowledge that their families in America would be ruined. It dawned on me that Dorothy would resort to any means to score. It dawned on me that she had planned her vengeance on Father for a long time. These angles took planning on her part. Moreover, it came to light that she'd taken crucial financial records from Father's office when she was doing summer bookkeeping for him years ago, and now, Father could not present those documents that would have supported his claims. All this and Dorothy knew the psychological power that her threat had on Jue Joe's old friends in Chinatown. I found her behavior nauseating.

I tell you this, Jack, with a heavy heart: To Aunt Dorothy the weak ones in the December of their lives always succumb. And everyone's weak, concludes her mental tally, if you know which buttons to push. In addition, the Land Title and Insurance Company is concerned over what this tiff might reveal regarding the exercises of its original cofounder, Otto F. Brant. So, its present spokesman is not inclined to testify on Father's behalf.

Observe with me Dorothy's courtroom theme. It goes like this, "Your Honor, Jue Joe did not leave a will, but he *intended* for me to have the Van Nuys ranch. He favored me. Yes, I own the Porterville property too, not my brother. You see, my brother works for me. He is my foreman on my Ranches."

Dorothy claimed that the Porterville ranch was a "gift" from Jue Joe to her and that Father was only the "trustee." In fact, Father had paid for the Porterville Ranch with his own savings, as I'd said to you earlier, but he couldn't produce the proof because Dorothy had taken care to derail his trail.

I know he's fleeced, my old man. This means working a street corner holding hat in hand. I can't imagine such empty wanderings yet to come. At twelve years old I hadn't seen much of the world. And I wasn't prepared for what would come.

In 1958, after Father lost his appeal, my mother spoke of the judge's verdict in this way: "Though your father is fifty-three years old he's still strong and healthy. We'll start over again. Your Aunt Dorothy didn't destroy him. Your father has us, and this is what's important. Your father is very talented, and he can do what he puts his mind to doing."

Skip to the year 1987. "Dorothy had no right to leave Father a pauper," said Jack Sr., my eldest brother. "She had no right to leave him nothing for his livelihood. He got nothing for all the sacrifice he'd made for the family."

We had come from Forest Lawn where Father lives now, six feet under. When he rises with the sun each morning, he can now view his beloved San Fernando Valley. And today, this day, his subtraction from our congress is profoundly felt by us all.

"I don't care how deep personal differences run," continued my brother Jack, "no one has the right to do what she did to him. Aunt Dorothy's intent was to rob his soul and to humiliate him and she succeeded. But in God's name—she had no right!"

Litigation had consumed our lives and our homestead shows it. One stroll around the Jue Joe Ranch in Van Nuys reveals to me the damage. The old packinghouse with its doors gone, with its eyes punched out, lay open to weather as if empty of thought. Only the creak and twist of wind is heard--a stale timbre bruising my soul. And in our yard amid weeds advancing the John Deere tractor aches with discontent on vacant earth, its torso sinks beyond my view, and its nose peels from the elements and from a wave of human neglect.

Today our barnyard animals are nervous. Sensing loss the cats withdraw, stealing away to the next ranch in the San Fernando Valley. Songbirds abandon trees that bear them no fruit. In formation they wing southward on the iron roll of greater winds. And the creatures in our chicken coop? Each will fill us one by one. But we'll stay our rooster because he's old. He's blind too. And he gets day and night all mixed up; he crows when moonbeams jolt his soul. But tonight, my mother will leave him his last supper: one bowl of rice. She'll leave his cage door open, too. She says to me, "…so that he can wander away to search his end like the rest of us." My mother's voice unveils her distress for this brittle yet enduring cock. Then I watch the cock's sightless courage jerk along the seam of the old De Celis wagon trail, turning his plumage toward a ranch that echoes with a pit bull barking. That's how you fade like the Valley's ranch culture that once was. That's how you hear the faint cry of an old coyote bend through the Valley's lost dreams.

But not our Thunder. In a corral, Jack Sr. 's horse Thunder splays his strength of character. He whips his neck up and back. He chords his muscles, too, impaling you to commute his sentence. Thunder seems to understand that he's been consigned to meet his maker. You see, in the old days glue came from the living. But old Thunder, well, he was a treasure in our family and so he was spared. Now, there were takers.

Thunder's egg-shaped eyes throw at me a dreadful start. He wants me to help him. I confess, his eyes burn hot sorrow for my betrayal. But we do, we must, we will, and we move on, I lie to myself. I can hardly bear to watch Thunder's fate. The beast reads for himself the sum of humanity: that mankind registers a primordial character far more intense than that of his animal cohorts. I see on Thunder's massive neck the ropes of panic; they wind round a bagged but very brave bully. The kicks and whirls wrought by this vibrating beast bring five men to him. Five men it takes to straddle Thunder's fierce pride, and five more men it takes to press him into a trailer sent by Mrs. Custer's Glue Factory.

That's how it was for Father, Jack Sr., Guy, Cousin Loon, and a remaining Mexican worker on our ranch. The sweating Thunder wouldn't subdue his nerve one low octave on the high score of fate. Six attempts, then ten, and the men vault Thunder into Mrs. Custer's steel womb. I can hear Thunder's jackal-screams from that cold dead womb. Thunder's fear is enormous for he'd entrusted his freedom to our family that embraced all strays. Now, he stands in close confine with Whitey, Joans's mare, laying lifeless on the floor of the steel trailer.

Poor old Thunder. I am not able to free myself from this Morgan stallion. Thunder's rage folds into the soft distance as I watch the steel trailer—harnessed to an Edsel—fade quickly from my horizon. In the days following Thunder's demise, I witnessed the power of a heartbreak. For the ghosts of time were pumping in my dreams.

I see Mama and Papa Kurihara bawling aboard the Star of Yokohama. From their deck amid bright-colored streamers they're waving white hankies to flag our eyes on the concrete dock below. At the Port of Los Angeles, we had elbowed through its enormous crowds. Now, Mama and Papa catch our sentiment as we begin to wave to them. How peculiar for me to catch this old, childless couple surrender to their fusillade of feelings as I've never seen in them. From the moment of my existence, they'd been in my life. Mama and Papa were the jewels fixed to the underside of our lives. In Jue Joe's cabin on our ranch they took to the rhythm of its country, and they distinguished this coordinate with collages of Japan.

It was like having a bit of village life come alive from the old places in our dreams. Thursdays and I would hear the fish man roar his green truck onto our gravel driveway. The fish man knew to toss Bingo a squid while Mother and Mama examined a rock cod. I knew that I would soon taste delectable pearls from the sea at supper time. To the fish man who spoke to me in single syllables, I was a prattler intensely off-key, for I gave him Japanese quite messed up. But truth be this: Mama would intervene on my behalf, she corrected my gibber and laughed so hard that her prune face broke into splints, then all I saw was a custard orifice and a donut of black hair. She floated folk songs down the character of my life and shuffled pigeon-toed on our kitchen floor in a dance that told me of faraway places. Mama was our housekeeper who brought to us Japan as in a doll's house, though Papa held Mama to his feudal ways. One day she wailed to my mother, "Papa go Downtown and he say to me, 'I go, you stay home!' Water fall down my eyes."

I tell you that Papa had a face squeezed of juices by his rising sun. Two rips wiggled beneath his brows, and he flashed you the biggest pair of ears you ever saw! They flapped forward as they pinned his face to the ground to catch an orchestra playing in our garden. Then I saw Papa shoot that music with DDT. Suddenly, white gardenias bloomed to perfume the grace of our broad front porch; irises drew their purple swords to guard our walkways of red brick; bushes of roses and hyacinths and camellias, columns of cypress trees, the curving green fur that licked along our ground—they grew up with the poetry of Papa. He was our gardener and he drove my siblings and I to and from school. Papa and Mama told me of their internment camp where no dreams drifted them forward in that world, except for a shudder heaved from a wind hurling down Heart Mountain in Wyoming.

I remind you that strays came to us in this way. And when World War II ended the old Japanese couple came to stay with us, having no way to restart their lives. They faced a public quite electrified by the storms of grievance. So, my father gave to Mama and Papa a free place to live in Jue Joe's cabin. They didn't have to work, he told them. They didn't have to pay rent, too. But soon, the old couple flexed their gnarled fingers: she in the house; he in the garden. Mama and Papa dreamed of returning to Japan; to their old life, the one before human equation had transposed that interlude into a giant mushroom cloud.

"I want to see Japan before the sun grows dark on us," said Papa, after Father told him that we'd lost our homestead to Dorothy. I begged Papa not to leave us, but he explained to me, "We are old and can only think of the passing of seasons now. We will not be more burden to your father. He shared his family with us, he shared his life, and this will always be a blessing to us."

I tell you that in the year of 1958, I couldn't see another harvest on the Jue Joe Ranch, not like the ones that I once knew. Not after Father's appeals in the courts had failed to ignite a judicial review. To me Papa's words weighed heavy, and I felt in my heart the last pluck of life we would share together. What would await Mama and Papa

Kurihara at the far reach of an Eastern sun? I couldn't conceive in my mind this couple existing beyond the familiar feel of our Western land. They understood the same bends in life as I, though I admit, I was the youngest in our tribe and undeveloped in character. Nevertheless, Mama and Papa acknowledged with pride my duration on the walls of their interiors. Last week they had pressed into my hand a teacup chipped in places along its brim. It was a piece of themselves, and it was a treasure to me. Respectfully, they bowed to me at their waists, and I saw two scalps forested by rods of silver. Mama and Papa worked into me a Shinto's grail from the depth of their rare spirits. Then Mama turned that chipped teacup clockwise and presented me with a final drink. I tasted her green brew delicate as the Meiji's moon. With reverence Papa produced a bowl of sticky, red-beaned rice.

"The color red means good luck," said Papa to me, and he made a gift to me of the hand-crafted bowl. It was the only treasure that the couple could give.

I can no longer see the *Star of Yokohama*. The dock stands empty of the Kurihara's Ship. But I can feel the Santa Ana winds whip across my face as I dart from the emptied dock.

"Over here!" shouts Father. He toots the car's horn, and he adds, "Come along, hurry."

Inside the Chrysler's smooth black spirit Father revs its engine. Seated next to him is my sister Pingileen. I remember that the Chrysler had replaced my father's Lincoln Zephyr the moment our family began to multiply; now, its gray wool interior folds me into silence as the car's wheels explode down the road and onto a freeway nervous with antic. I think of ranch episodes vanishing as I see Downtown Los Angeles' lean skyscrapers flash by in shards of autumn sunlight. Soon, the Chrysler's wheels meet open space, and our ride turns swift. At once I think about the weight of what had passed at the dock. And I realize that I'm now shivering, for the heater in our Chrysler is on the blink and it will never know a repair.

On the Jue Joe Ranch, Grandma checks in at seventy years of age and I know this is a consecration held higher than the Himalayas. It enters the realm of the sacred because, at Grandma's age, you gain highest respect whether you've known any respect in your life or not. And if you acquire more seasons, you receive this highest respect every ten years in the same way. There is a banquet with special foods to celebrate your long life, and you are surrounded by all the generations in your family.

Last week my mother drove me to Frank Palmer Grant's Red Goose Shoe Store in Valley Market Town. We went to the strip mall because I wanted to find a new pair of shoes for Grandma's 70th birthday party tonight. Valley Market Town skirts a newly paved Van Nuys Boulevard, and town fathers had voted to upscale the image of Van Nuys. So, at the other end of Van Nuys Boulevard, away from our mart, they blasted concrete round 'til the Broadway Department Store rose two floors high. It boasted of having an escalator. The only one in the Valley. But our Valley Market Town wouldn't give it up. Instead, it held steadfast to its image as our best neighborhood general store: hardware, fresh produce stands, mom- and-pop stores, and my favorite Red Goose Shoe Store. It didn't forget ranch culture.

I tell you that Red Goose Shoe Store put up fierce competition: I shoved my new pair of chukkas into a machine that had a viewer and that caught my green toes wiggling in an X-ray. Frank Palmer's "shoe-fit fluoroscope" told my mother and I that the new shoes were a proper fit. But what excited me about coming to the Red Goose Shoe Store was its makeshift zoo: a baby alligator parked in front of the Store's entrance. A live one. Although it lay tranquilized by the Valley's summer heat. The baby gator was caged in chicken wire and children begged their moms to bring them to see this noble wonder at the Red Goose Shoe Store.

Torchlights throw their glow round our big swimming pool on the Ranch. In our bathhouse I smell roast pig suckling on a spit in our brick BBQ fireplace. Below the rotating pig, and buried in red embers, sweet ears of corn wrapped in foil flick their fumes up in air. A cackle of logs in the belly of Grandma's black-iron stove roils a kettle steeping on its disk, its spout whistles with feeling. Grandma's stove had gained new status as a treasured antique when it transferred from her old cottage to Father's newly built bathhouse; here, it would oversee an extended family's milestones. But in our bathhouse readied for Grandma's birthday—she cannot eat. She has a chemistry problem.

This is how a doctor had read her yesterday. Tapping her exposed chest, his fingers worked her hide like a grim archaeologist. Then he straightened his torso. He crossed his arms over his chest, which stirred in me a picture of a pelican pausing in a winter's pond. I heard his beak move to opine on Grandma's condition.

"…and she'll need to be watched very closely," voices the doctor. His fuss continues, "It's her high blood pressure, she might have another stroke. Has she passed her kidney stones yet? She is still weak from her last operation and…."

Scorched by the fires of time Grandma feeds on Gerber's baby food. She can't chew; the dentures keep slipping. And she is due for more medical care. I see that she is growing very pale. I see my father weighted by concern for her. He knows that he must act with swiftness.

So, they came to agreement, my father, and my Aunt Corrine. But their phone conversation had been hard, accusing. I remember thinking: a quarter of a century will pass before the shards of a broken family reconnect again. What was that Chinese proverb? Oh yes, it runs this way, "…the whole in time heals its injured parts…." This is what my father believed; it anchored itself deep in his interior. But I wondered if I could ever find in myself the courage to forgive and to believe in the whole.

Returning from Hong Kong, Aunt Corrine and Uncle Lansing settled in San Mateo in northern California. Uncle Lansing was now running Wing On's international trading company from an office in San Francisco, California.

The hard truth for Father? Now, he had no money for the family's medical care—even for Grandma. Should old folk be told of this humiliating truth? Father looked distraught.

We had exchanged one continent for another, but such exchange had brought to us an exacting price. I remember Father seated at a kitchen table. He had one elbow braced on the tabletop as he studied Grandma who was seated directly across from him. She had finished her rice porridge. With a pained voice he said to her, "Ma, you have a good visit with Corrine in San Mateo. And when you've had a fine rest up there, you come home, o.k.?" He helped his mother rise slowly from her chair, he gave her a big hug and planted a kiss on her snowy hairline.

"Corrine told me she gonna take you to San Francisco's Chinatown for dinner," continues Father. "You haven't been there since we come over, you remember?" Grandma Leong Shee had to stop and think. "The air was chilly then," reminds Father. "It was foggy too. Then a strong wind come up, snagged everything standing in its way." Father's words painted for his mother a postcard of February youth.

"Where's Jackie?" replies Leong Shee looking for her grandson, Jack Sr.. "He has my coat. I need my wool coat." It's a warm summer morning in Van Nuys, but Old San Francisco flicks across her mind and enlarges a scratch of memory.

"Jackie's packed your winter coat," replies Father. "It's all in the car, all loaded—"

"What are you trying to tell me, Son?"

"I'm telling you that Corrine's flying in tomorrow to pick you up at Dorothy's house. But you'll be back with me on the ranch in no time, Ma, because this is your home, right here, this will always be your home. Now, Ma...don't Cry, Ma...no one's throwing you out. We have done this for your own good. Your health is what's most important. And Jackie's packed a few things that you'll need for San Francisco. He's waiting for you outside in the car. C'mon, Ma, I'll help you to the car."

Jack Sr. darted in and out of our old Chrysler. The hood of the trunk swung up and every space was filled with Grandma's seersucker dresses. In the Car's backseat I saw her belts, shoes, bathrobe for winter, and one for summer. And her woolly coat. I saw her Chinese relics from the Old World, each infused with exotic wonder: a large loop-handled scissor that used to cut one new garment once a year for her two young sons, San You and San Tong. There was a fish-boned comb that had sailed with her from Sum Gong Village. Pungent aroma still sailed from her sandalwood fan. And I touched for one last time Grandma's teakwood idols. Finally, I covered the lids on her tin cans, now corroding from herbs aging and the hint of a forgotten world on the other side of time.

In the cloister of that Chrysler, Jack made space for Grandma's view. Then I watched her countenance expand across the width of the Car's glass window, and as she swivelled around for one last look at us, her lips began to stretch like rubber bands upon which railed the years of her mighty tears. Then I heard the Chrysler's ignition falter then rise as Jack pumped its pedal, and noise roared, and a family's heartbreak drowned in that spare and fleeting moment. The Car's wheels buried then exploded down the old De Celis trail and onto Vanowen Street, which was now paved so that the iron chariot roared away in smooth silence. I knew the sleek Chrysler would cut for Dorothy's house in Coldwater Canyon. I knew in my heart that we would never see Grandma again.

As the Chrysler vanished, my heart swelled for the emptied yard in Father's interior. A corona of utter sadness engulfed him; it showed me a being involuntarily indentured to the reality of his life. A very special dream had died for him, and I saw his shoulders begin to heave with untold tears of suffering.

"Get back!" shouts my father to my mother, as he zigzags away from our lit trash hole, the one dug between our bathhouse and our packinghouse. It swallows all scraps of lost reward. My mother sees my father flushed with anger, and she says to him, "…but I, I thought it was just papers in that box and—"

Bullets from the trash hole tear the air. Within minutes the sound is followed by sirens exploding from an iron posse. Great red machines halt on our gravel driveway in a swirl of dust and hot anxiety.

"Oh gosh," flails Father. Tanked spirit steals his soul, a fire chief steps from the red iron and onto the Jue Joe Ranch. The fire chief throws Father a look as if he'd pinched an arsonist. The big asbestos-ladened man steps back to scan overgrown weeds on our Ranch waving back at him. I'd hoped the chief would see the Ranch's tall character; instead, he noted to Father that this was an unlicensed fire trap. I watch the chief register on paper what he then gives to Father: a something or other bereft of care.

"But we've been forced to vacate this premise," explains Father to the fire chief. He shows the asbestos-ladened man Aunt Dorothy's "Notice of Eviction."

The fine is stiff for an illegal burning. I linger at the trash hole and see nettles wandering oddly through the air, and I realize that Jue Joe Ranch had passed in a wink and something else would be coming. But my family and I weren't a part of its new style. As such, we gave Regulators their purpose in life.

The rope snaps on our twelve-foot-long freezer; it flies the blue whale down our basement's wooden stairs to land where it had lived for years as an arctic king. The men had used blocks ripped from a bedframe on which Lupe's mattress once laid—in the basement—to stay the whale from slippage. But the freezer resisted all efforts of the men: my father, my brothers, my cousin, my brothers-in-law to be. And now, the freezer sat motionless on top of blocks splayed at the bottom of the stairs.

"Oh, Lupe," I notify the wind, "you don't have your bed no more." Lupe had vanished like the other Mexicans on the Jue Joe Ranch to become rips of light in the distance of my memory. Nevertheless, her jolly presence is still with me.

"How come you got no little finger?" threw my query at Lupe. We were in the basement of our house where she lived. Lupe helped with household chores after Grandma had suffered a stroke and needed my mother's care. Now, I marvelled at Lupe's missing socket on her right hand. "How come you don't have that finger," I pumped again. Lupe laughed in loops, which made her large breasts ripple in great waves.

"My boyfriend," leaped Lupe's return, "he slam car door on me one night. Accident, yes? But my boyfriend he faint from fright. I feel no pain, so I wave down taxi and go see doctor."

Make no mistake. Lupe's mustache lover pined for her forgiveness. In a lather of guilt, the guy squared up. He tied the knot and retrieved her heart at the marriage altar.

Today we move from the Jue Joe Ranch. This is the rub. What we don't bring to our new abode, but intend to return in the morning to fetch, is stolen from us during the night: doors, windows, tools, machinery—and Father's camper. Father had pieced together his camper from scratch. It was meant to be a new start for him, for us. And it was to carry him and Cousin Loon across the prairie and into gator country. Meaning Florida's Everglades in which he had a plan to start us over. On the Jue Joe Ranch a few rows of asparagus had refused to whither, too, they were the ones that Father had saved from human edit by posting, "No Trespass." Overnight, the rows were scalped. Only stumps told you that life had once lived here.

Wednesday. I hear my mother's urgent summons to my siblings and me. We gather in the upstairs bedroom of my parents. There, enormous pain pounds across my mother's face. It is an agony as I'd never seen in her. She bears the weight of no tomorrows as her finger points to a spot on their rose-colored, silk bedspread.

"Yesterday morning your father locked himself in our bedroom," opens my mother's lips. She tamps his tumbling ache down our souls, "...and, and all day he wept by himself. All day! I want you to see how your father's heart let go. Look there, his tears. Look at them and understand what the loss of our homestead means to your father."

O my god! informs my interior. The dark shape that I see tamped on their bedspread is bigger than a man's head! It takes a torrent of tears to map and fill a lake like this, I notify myself.

"I want you to understand what your father feels but cannot express aloud," continues my mother. Her voice is sprained, exhausted, bombarded by an unspeakable burden. For the wideness of Father's inner sea overran my character, too. So enormous was his heartbreak. It was one man's soul exploding from the myriad of treasons heaped on him. I felt helpless in my ability to reach my father to comfort him. I felt terrified. I had never experienced the depth of my father's emotions, not like this, for in public he never allowed himself such unravelling. It is considered an act of weakness for a man, according to Chinese custom. This was my father San Tong's point of view. This was his father Jue Joe's point of view. This was canon laid down for all sons of China. But here lay the stain of irrevocable rupture before my eyes. Father let go and cried centuries of sorrow to only a rose-colored bedspread that could not comfort him.

My father gave way to the loss of something deeper than an immigrant's worn-out dream. He felt the core of his existence—all that he believed in—take an uncontrollable turn, and he had not understood himself inside that twist of fate. To Father, the condition of unity was the fabric of our family's consciousness. And no matter what its deficiencies, he felt that this unity could not be questioned. Grounding gave to Father the validity of this belief. I watched attempts to restart his life begin to misfire, as old men in their desperate hour often face. Nevertheless, Father brought up great courage that reinforced his ability to take those blows. I grew to love my old man and to respect him even more for his character that carried him through life with such spirit.

As we departed the Jue Joe Ranch, I closed our massive white front door. Before its face carved with the character of *fook,* which means "good fortune," my finger traced the grooves of that character. I wondered if that bronzy character knew the irony of a river's journey down the lea of dreams. Long ago, Father had stood before the character of *fook* and had pointed to me its soul-cry, he said to me, "Do you see the *fook?* It means good fortune! There is power in this word, and it will bring to us many good years, you wait and see." He smiled at me, and he believed.

A coyote's cry bends through a valley, and you hear it no more. A valley blooms with green pastures, and you see that valley no more. Now, I see track homes hoop-roll across the San Fernando Valley. In Northridge, our new home sits among that jolly. The pressures of autumn pile upon our senses, and I confess, moving to this new place was a costly affair. Slapped with Dorothy's Notice of Eviction, my father didn't know which way to turn. So, he kept us together on the Jue Joe Ranch for as long as he could. He kept us there so that I—his youngest child—could graduate from Birmingham High School, which was only a short walk from our Ranch.

When lawmen came to the Ranch to enforce Dorothy's Notice of Eviction, Father had politely bid on a track house that was up for sale and that was south of our property. It was land that had once been a part of Jue Joe Ranch, but in March of 1950, had been sold to Southwest Properties, Inc., for subdivision. I remember that the owner of this yellow house whose front lawn languished in weeds, said to my father, "I don't sell to no Chinks!" Then the beer-bellied Anglo slammed the door in Father's face. There was no escape, I thought, from an old storm colliding with our destiny.

I tell you, Jack, for days my father roiled with ulcers from the meanness of that man. But finally, another owner stepped forward. He was willing to peddle his house to a

Chinaman. This owner, you see, was a Jew who comprehended convolutions in the human equation. And the Jew's home on Shoshone Avenue in Northridge warmed our hope for a new start. Nevertheless, it was strange for me to turn around and bump into a neighbor living next door; on the Jue Joe Ranch, our closest neighbor was a mile away. This new lifestyle in Northridge I had yet to get acquainted with.

In my old life, I walked a mile across open fields to visit a pioneer granny. Her name was Mrs. White, and she rang sleigh bells from a horn on her Model T pickup. That's how I knew when Mrs. White was nearing our Ranch. She piloted her tin jalopy like a racer down the old De Celis wagon trail.

Jolly Mrs. White worked a busted clutch on her Model T, and you heard the motor cough and you saw patches of gray paint oxidizing, peeling. But she worked that iron horse to come shower my siblings and I with Santa Claus' treasures: fairytale storybooks, animal storybooks, they were Winter's joy wrapped in a rainbow of ribbons. Mrs. White was part of a ranch culture that embraced all strays and whatnots in the San Fernando Valley. And if you followed the dusty DeCelis trail to her cottage, you saw that it was filled with simple enchantment. You saw that it was in fact a magical world: she possessed a Victorian doll collection that would make a serious collector swoon. These delicate dolls lived on her shelves from floor to ceiling and all around her living room. Each porcelain face pulsated with joy that swept round the cottage and that sprang from Mrs. White.

But in our new existence there was a big query, could we make next month's house payment? We could not. So, Father made his way South of the Border to drum for work. The rest of us in Northridge rolled the Relief Worker. Confucius says that inside one's failure, real courage begins. Well, this was a daily challenge.

"All I want is to be able to cook for my family," wept my mother Ping to the Relief Worker. Bedridden, she disrobed her deformed hands for him to see, hands that incubated life's inexpiable distortions. The Relief Worker pulled out his hanky and blew his nose and the following week a wheelchair arrived for my mother.

How I remember what Father always taught us. He said it again when he was home for a visit from Mexico: "There are three levels of truth that you must learn, my children, in understanding the contours of the human character. It is called *'hao yip sum choong.'* And it means the following: The face of human character tells you nothing unless you seek the depth behind that face and unless you carefully examine its facets by using your interior eye. This brings you to the second level. But your knowledge of character on this second level is insufficient, even though you think you know it, because you have not determined the true motives behind that human character. Only after you've dug down all the way will you know the inner clock of those who roam the human contest. And this, my children, is the third level that you must learn."

Father's think tank was all that he had to give us. The Relief Worker, on the other hand, sent us food stamps. But truth be this. Two halves defined the life of my father. The one before Dorothy's lawsuit; and the one afterward.

Blue surf, pearly beach, a thatched cafe sitting idle on that beach, this was a fishing village called "La Paz" nestled at the tip of Baja California. In that café in which mariachi musicians had long evaporated, Father stayed his presence and penned a letter to my mother Ping in Northridge, California.

"You can find some grace in this far-away setting," wrote Father. His interior opened wide to Ping, "La Paz is a strangely beautiful place. It's filled with all kinds of mood swings. It's to the liking of old men with smells of time lingering on their breath. What I've seen is quite diverse: a town set alive by poor inhabitants propelling pushcarts; American expats sailing on the bay, fishing, living on pensions; and local politicians and military men buying up villas and towns. La Paz itself remains pristine as a rugged dream.

"I'm staying at the Purisima Hotel for the time being, where there's a horse-drawn surrey parked outside its iron gate. It takes guests on tours. I'm gonna take you for a ride around the Square in that surrey when you come visit me, Ping.

"You won't believe this, but yesterday I ran into Ramon Navarro. Remember him? He's Ritchie Valens' stepfather, so to speak. Ramon told me that he lives in La Paz now. He's very old and nearly blind and says he left Connie and the kids years ago in the San Fernando Valley. He got caught and was deported. He wandered round for some time, but finally, he's come home to La Paz to spend his remaining days by the sea.

"From this cafe on the beach I see the lights of fishing boats, too, they are returning to shore as evening is approaching. But in the water, sharks know that fishermen in small boats lash their biggest fish to the sides of their boats, and these sharks track those boats for the day's catch. A few Americans have now entered this café, Ping. I know that they are down here thinking of ways to restart their lives. It's those small ideas spinning around in dreams that bring a big tomorrow. I want this for us, too, Ping."

There was no living and there was no dying for Father. Instead, there was a melancholy void so deep in him that a soul must make a dream, or else, a man like Father would have no purpose, no way to live! His idea of America—the green rolling hills and fields of Uncle Sam—had passed down a vortex and into oblivion. He could not boot himself into America's new facsimile of character, not at his age, for family farms in America had forked over a last breath, and in its place, Agri conglomerates grew glass-and-steel profits on a scale unimaginable.

In Mexico, Father groped for the content of his spirit and this treasure he mailed to his six children every month. He used carbon sheets of paper to multiply his visions, pounding out feeling on a portable, WWII Olympia typewriter. Through his visions, I forged a montage of his enormous suffering. And the rotating events from his pen scratched at my heart. I heard a soul pounded by life's exhaustions, but I caught his credence in which fear and self-doubt began to fail against his solitary will.

In the San Fernando Valley, she is alone. She grows sick. I see my mother's joints and knuckles swell. They turn dark. When she brings her fingers into light they are gnarled like a gnome's. And those fingers used to strum for me Canton solos on her butterfly harp; the harp that had sailed with her from the old country and that was a child-bride's things. I see my mother Ping's fingers through which a cup, a plate, a bowl, slips to shatter on the kitchen floor. The joints in her fingers no longer work for her. She remains in constant pain because she had refused medical treatment so that we, in her mind, could meet our monthly household expenses. Confined to her bed, Ping is a prisoner of musty idea. No, no, she is a guardian of brave idea. In her bedroom there are four blank walls for her to stare at, walls on which to screen the unfulfilled dreams of her life. And below the wallpaper's rude stains she knows that a wheelchair—which the Relief Worker had sent her—adorns her enclosure as a useless display.

For Ping cannot rise to reach her wheelchair, but she can feel a hush growing round her. She can feel soft carpets beneath her silky womb, and the stilled rumblings of her small range. At once Ping knows this is a chamber exploding with florals and their sweet-smelling aromas. A familiar breeze takes her, she can feel her husband San Tong bend to kiss her face. But her casing is now cold and hard as rock, she tries to inform him. Then she feels her husband move sadly away to join their children seated in a pew behind her casket. She hears music begin to flow in this small white chapel at Forest Lawn Cemetery.

My father unveils an intensity that I've never seen before. I watch a cascade of great feeling roll onto his sun-browned hands in that pew. They are endless tear drops tapping forever on hands that reap a harvest of sorrow. For no other sound emits from him but the boom-gong of those great big drops.

This I remember.

CHAPTER 10 – FAMILY BONDS

A monsoon parts its pleat and a woman appears with a child strapped to her back. Bullets cut around her. A hundred boots give her chase. The sticky air glues a pair of black pajamas to her young hide. Suddenly, lead ruptures the air to force this mother and her child off Jue Joe's rooftop in the Village of Sum Gong. She takes to the interior of his house. But boots continue their sweep down the hutongs of Sum Gong, which are nameless alleys winding round old lore and which today kowtow to a new reality: the children of Sum Gong lob a deadly charge at the marching boots—they unleash their sticks and stones. Yes that. For Sum Gong Village had prayed for armored whatnots from the authorities but found itself taken by vigilantes claiming membership in the new Red Army.

Earlier, San Tong Jue's cousin Mansui had fled from the Town of Sun Wui where she found a torso, a head, and pieces of her husband splayed in crimson on the main drag. Her husband, the palms merchant of Sun Wui, mottled the roadside like minced tofu. Banging with panic, Mansui hoisted her little girl onto her back and tore for the foot of Snake Mountain, in Sum Gong Village, to seek refuge in Jue Joe's abode. In particular, she took to her father Jue Shee's attached library in which books of knowledge rocketed round her about safe havens in other worlds.

"Where are they?" she informs herself. Mansui means the deeds to Jue Joe's family compound that he had built in 1903. For she and her father were the caretakers of Jue Joe's ancestral lands after he had sailed to California in 1906. She was promoted up a score after Leong Shee and her two sons had sailed to join him in 1918. This is because the practice of caretaking in China is an ancient custom designed to keep a family together as an economic and social unit. Every member has a duty to maintain the whole.

Right here, it's here. Jue Joe's deeds lay upstairs in his flushing toilet. This is where Leong Shee had hidden his deeds so long ago. Mansui reaches for the yellowed scrolls and brings them onto Jue Joe's balcony for a better read. At once silver pellets cut around her as Jue Shee, her father, appears below with a lead pipe foisted upward at her. He unloads his trusty equalizer at a frigate, or so he thinks.

"Papa don't shoot—It's me!" shouts Mansui in panic.

Poor poor Jue Shee. His beef is inward, so scrambled is his aged brain that he aims again at a *Namikaze* destroyer. He pats the air's canvas for a flag of a Bygone Order, feels none, then hears himself signal aloud his impudence. More volleys explode. The barrel misfires, stamping from history an old man's soul.

That was then, this is now.

Mansui hears Red Army boots march closer. In Sum Gong Village's big canal, her treacherous journey begins. As the liquid womb absorbs her feet, then her legs and torso, brine blows from Mansui's nostrils as she feels her legs surrender to peristaltic action. Around the curves of Sum Gong's tea-stained sluice she slides, hoisting her toddler high above her head to keep the girl dry. Mansui's short legs tread like the turbine of a John Deere tractor, though in time pain shoots from her legs up to her throat. Gong-cries strafe the waves of the big canal; the cries grow deafening. They are brittle voices that scream for help in the big canal as Mansui streaks past those ancients of Sum Gong Village. These old-timers command no strength to survive a civil war ranting, and they sink into oblivion in Neptune's world. But Mansui cannot stop to feel for the old ways. It is every woman for herself. For instinct overruns moral scripture as gunboats gain advantage.

A shock of light lands upon Mansui's toddler poised above the breakers. The light paces the little girl held above water with pinpoint accuracy. Mansui dives with her child like a porpoise, she leaps for air and dives again. She feels her child eject sea-brine at each leap for air. She hears her child wail in terror at those intervals. On this note Mansui begs the heavens for forgiveness.

Next day, mother and daughter drift down a channel that gunboats had forgotten. Divested of rage this blue fabric provides the pair with a stroke of calm. The dawn reveals to Mansui healthy shrubs shellacked with dew along a riverbank. The stillness gives Mansui pause to assess her moment. For the first time since the siege on Sum Gong Village had begun, Mansui put aside her scissor-kicks. She put aside her bale of anguish as she plucks at shrubs, tearing off the most tender blades for her child to chew.

Soon Mansui flows into major conjunction. She and her child eddy into the essence of foreign risk. Gray ships glide silently across a congested harbor, bearing flags of many nations. From their decks the sailors in white salute a skyline's chaos: overhead walkways on which sleek suits shuffle from those steel arteries and into enterprises that look over-built.

These are canyons of upscale persona, notes Mansui's interior, that seem to heave with nervousness. Meaning eclectic turbines of fishing trolls that dock, that depart, that cross in a blink—Victoria Harbor. It's the sights and sounds of human energy that feed the coined pyramids of Hong Kong. And Hong Kong never sleeps lest you forget her existence. Over here the freighters swollen with pilings of Malay timber dock at Kuai Chung Harbor. Over there a passenger liner spews the content of its world into Hong Kong's inviting tentacles.

By the Star Ferry, Mansui stops to watch a vendor with a pushcart. He tongs beef satay onto bamboo skewers, which a mob aroused to frenzy storms. On the edge of broken pavement, she examines sidewalk culture too: a butcher blowtorches pig's feet on the broken pavement. He tosses the singed hooves into a wheelbarrow. A cook from a cafe around the corner approaches him, their fingers throw scissors and hammers, their voices rise to otherworldly screams. Finally, the smoking hooves are lurched away in that wheelbarrow by the cook.

Grannies toting plastic bags filled with whatnots rudely elbow their way up a ferry's gangplank, and once onboard, they see hordes of office workers in designer suits stay their positions on wooden benches. It's no use. In Mansui's interior, scenes like these are alien to the life she once knew in Sum Gong Village. For slow-motion dreams of village folk have no equivalent to speed-dial action blasting headlines across the *South China Morning Post.*

"I must remember the house," informs Mansui to herself. "The address that Cousin San Tong had once told me...I gotta know, know how to get there."

On Hong Kong Island a limousine glides up toward Village Road. It takes a hairpin turn and throws a lady seated in the back against the car's glass window, leaving a morose impression on her mind. The limo runs a switchback. It cuts another sharp turn. What sails from the lady's jewelled fingers is a letter that she'd been reading.

Corrine rescues the letter off the car's floor as her interior rewinds a thought about its handwriting: to imagine her brother San Tong's urgency and worry, why, life on the Jue Joe Ranch seems to her a distant memory. Comfort patrols Corrine's interior, and San Tong's anguish brings to her a bale of discontent. At once Corrine feels the "old burden" like a crick; a thing she didn't want to revisit. After all, life in Hong Kong had been a means of escape, and, indeed, she wasn't about to mess up. This is because her life's journey up the twisting road with her husband Lansing Kwok had secured for her a grace far from a rural family's outhouse brawls, so to speak.

Corkscrewing up Happy Valley's roads toward Fung Fai Terraces, Corrine's limo passes squatters' huts that creep too close for her repose. But the tin roofs with cardboard sides soon give way to mansions perched on sidewalls of Happy Valley that throw a daring point of view: Hong Kong at nightfall is a blink of sapphires and there's no other counterpoint in the world that is as vibrant as this little gem.

The limo's chauffeur rounds a sharp turn to the right off Village Road, he swings up a narrow driveway to Fung Fai Terraces, stopping abruptly at a massive front door. To the young driver on the job for only two days, Corrine conveys her personal urgency, "…and bring more chairs from the balcony for my dinner guests. They must be seated properly. I cannot emphasize this enough to you… (blah blah blah)."

The massive front door bolts open, and a teenage girl appears in uniform. Her jet hair is roped into two slave-balls, one on each side of her head. Corrine explains to her maid, "Come with me quickly, unpack these boxes. Hurry now, they'll be here soon."

In the dining room a grandfather clock chimes. It prompts Corrine and her maid to scan their eyes down a long table. Frowning, Corrine revs her throttle, "This color table linen is wrong. Change those florals. The napkin rings must match, you know." Corrine leaves her maid to wander through a woodland of entangled worries.

Upstairs in the master bedroom, Corrine is struck by sunset waning through a picture window. Flickers of silver light carpet Victoria Harbor below, and the scene draws Corrine onto her balcony and into the evening's sultry air. A gust of breeze bends through the falling day. Hong Kong. What a magical world it is, she feels.

When neon lights wink, a humanity of shoes ensues from tall buildings. They putter down frenetic sidewalks. At day's end, they bid good-bye to foreign commotion; welcome a moonlight to polish their souls. Corrine, on the other hand, snaps open Hong Kong's royal registry. It's the wives of the Jockey Club members in Happy Valley who will honor her with their presence tonight at her home on Fung Fai Terrace.

"Madam, someone is here to see you," conveys her maid.

"Already?" gasps Corrine in disbelief. Hong Kongers should arrive properly late, informs her interior. After all, this is Chinese custom. They should be late so as not to appear rude, not to show too much zest for pigging out.

"Very well," laments Corrine, "show my guests to the parlor."

"Madam, she don't look like a guest. I ask her to come back in morning, but she wants to see you. Come look, Madam." The maid with two slave-balls draws Corrine to the big picture window, and says, "Down in front she stand. You see her?"

A black wad stoops to adjust rags piled on her back. Her hair is cut in a bowl-shape and pushed behind the ears. Corrine sees in the evening's ray an unexplained stray.

Mansui calls up to Corrine, "Cousin! Cousin Corrine!" Her black pajamas flap against a humid breeze. She feels her baby kick in her arms, and in quickness cranks again, "It's me, Cousin, it's M—"

"Use the back door to the kitchen—quickly!" blocks Corrine, her index-finger points Mansui to a yellow door hidden round the home's side; it's a narrow vent that ushers in the help. Corrine glances down her street and records with relief that her neighbors had not seen this stray enter her home.

Days later Corrine addresses Mansui, "...and, and these people will help find you a place to stay." Light penetrates through Corrine's kitchen window. "I've already notified my brother San Tong on the Jue Joe Ranch in Van Nuys, and he'll send you money."

British gray. The Red Cross look. On Hong Kong's waterfront stands a 1911-built warehouse that hands Mansui a miracle. It can happen if you believe in miracles. And in Hong Kong everyone invests in this mysterious wonder. After Mansui had settled in a Christian Charity House, she storms the Red Cross Annex next door. She has faith that amid the ruined faces that flood the Annex every day—arriving in rowboats and floating baskets and fleeing war—she will find a champion among staff to help her emigrate to

America. She pats her pocket for Cousin San Tong's cash that's pinned to its underside. It's still safe. Relieved, Mansui's mind scans the vastness of the rank-smelling Annex. A roar of acreage, this certainly is. For a roster of orphans in that Annex grows by leaps and bounds as Civil War in China rears its character uncontrolled.

Up and down the Cat Alleys of Hong Kong, mother and child become the endless queue of faces foraging for food, seeking shelter, waiting for a life that refuses to deliver to them a secure footing.

…and a DC-10 flies westward across the wide Pacific. It shoves the content of Mansui's stomach into a doggy bag. A lady seated next to her does not react. Instead, the lady's sleep-shade pinches her blond hair into crazy quills. This American seems misplaced, informs Mansui's interior, until she captures the fact that in this pressurized cabin, she alone is the curiosity nestled in First Class. The lady asleep and seated next to Mansui is her sponsor who'd selected this refugee for emigration to New York City. Mansui would serve this kind American woman. However, unable to bring her baby girl with her, Mansui leaves the child at a missionary house in Hong Kong until she can earn enough money to send for her; until she can learn how to navigate legal rigmarole in America. The long hours bending through space relaxes Mansui. She prays that the place this bird wings her toward is not a replay of the world she left behind.

Drifting to sleep Mansui conjures a flag waving in air. American? But what is it that moves? Is it the wind that moves? Or is it the flag? To Mansui it is neither, but only the mind that really moves. It moves her towards the reality of him. She remembers her cousin San Tong as a tall man. A man with serious eyes who had come from America to Jue Shee's library decades ago. San Tong had come to marry Yee Lai Ping, a young bride from the Town of Sun Wui, which is situated an hour north of Sum Gong Village in the Pearl River delta. Mansui recalls that Cousin San Tong and his new bride fled quickly to Jeongmen Harbor because the Japanese Navy had hoisted its flag above the Harbor. It would soon be blockaded. Jeongmen Harbor, she knew, was the only entry and exit to and from the Pearl River delta. So, there was no futzing around. San Tong's ship had to run a Japanese blockade.

The DC-10 opened its landing gear as Manhattan below grew larger through Mansui's window; the expanding pelt below jolted alive as the bird's wheels hit the tarmac. At once Mansui registered one wish in her interior: I will find Cousin San Tong in California and reunite with the family.

In the Lower East Side of Manhattan, noise strangled the air and traffic pushed Mansui into a garment shop. The owner, husband of the nice lady who sponsored Mansui, offered the latter ten cents by the piece. Seven days a week Mansui foot-pumped an old, so very old Singer sewing machine. And each week she stuffed her dime-store socks with Uncle Sam's silver treasures. In a tiny room in Chinatown, which boasted of a communal privy, Mansui in time stashed away enough dough to send for her teenage daughter whom she had left at a Jesus house in Hong Kong many years ago.

And now, now at seventy-eight years old, Mansui is traveling to see Cousin San Tong whom she last saw in her father's library in 1937, in Sum Gong Village. She was only sixteen years old, chuckles her once youthful self. What will this reunion be like? The Greyhound bus lumbers her query away from pedestrians flying a busy intersection in New York City. Then flat open space trundles her mind down seams that zigzag across America. Finally, the steel rocker works Mansui down California's Grapevine Pass and into the San Fernando Valley.

"It's so good to see you," voices Fay Loon, who is the widow of Cousin Sik Loon and who is my mother Ping's older sister too. She had invited Mansui to stay with her in the city of Reseda, which is west of Van Nuys in California. "We have changed since I last saw you in Hong Kong, Mansui. It seems a lifetime ago, doesn't it?" The pain of living addresses the two women in their golden years as Fay continues, "After Ping's funeral, I asked San Tong, 'May I step over a lighted candle for my sister tonight? This is the right thing to do for her.'"

Let me pause to tell you, Jack, that in Chinese custom, stepping over a lighted candle on the first night that follows a funeral releases the spirit of a deceased person to the cosmic realm. This is tradition.

"'No, no, don't do this!' replied San Tong. Just like that. He's changed I tell you. And you won't recognize him as you didn't my own face. We're the shadows of our youth, though I admit that as I opened my front door, I knew immediately that it was you, Mansui. You're still a ball of vigor. But you've travelled far and long, you rest now and tomorrow we'll go see San Tong. Last week he came home from Mexico to visit his children. He rotates from house to house. Did you know this? And life I hope has been good to you?"

Fay Loon brings Mansui to our home in Northridge to see her cousin San Tong.

"You looked so spiffy in your Panama hat, do you remember?" The corners of Mansui's eyes unfold their fan-wrinkles. The club of her arm falls short of reaching her tall cousin's imaginary hat. She says to San Tong, "And so handsome...*hmm...*you've not changed in all these years." She lied.

Make no mistake. Hear a coyote call and dry winds of the San Fernando Valley bend in those aimless moves; the Santa Ana's breath is riddled with primal mood swings. Today, it darts through a window of our Northridge home to snap a shot of Mansui's gold tooth as she laughs joyfully in the morning's flare. She reveals to Cousin San Tong her good-natured inclination. Mansui's pie-shaped face slices off humour. But then she bombards her cousin with questions: What happened? Why are you in Mexico? What are you doing down there? What happened to the Jue Joe Ranch? Why did you have to move?

Words that club. Words that are a reminder of certified failure, feels San Tong. He gropes for a genteel reply. But strife festers to bang round his interior. He explodes, "You mean leading our band into exile and now we're lost?"

No answer takes the moment. The lack of idea wears on San Tong's heart like a grate of iron. His lips mince away Mansui's fellowship. He continues, "For years I've toiled for this family while not fingering anything for myself. And you know where that has left me? South of the Border plucking cactus. I have lost what means so much to me, Mansui, the family. And my whole life's work—all of it—was ripped away from me. I have nothing. Look at my own flesh and blood, my sisters, will you? They did what was unthinkable—they destroyed the family. They, they think they've got their safe places that seem enough horizon for them. I took care of Corrine and Dorothy like my own children; gave them a good schooling and all. But they wanted more, especially Dorothy. She wanted what I couldn't give her: freedom from the anger that festered within herself and that she so willingly directed at me. Where her anger comes from, I just don't know. But it hurts the way she disregarded our parents' hardships. It hurts the way she disrespected my sacrifice for the well-being of our family. Her hate became so toxic. And for a time, I felt bum cracked up. But I can't look back. No, I won't let Dorothy's betrayal destroy me."

Father was feeling his desert. In his golden years he was floundering with no grip on a good season to throw it in reverse. He'd knocked on all kinds of doors, no, no, pounded on them desperately in the hope that one would open and spread before him a miracle: that his present situation was only an illusion. He would make a comeback. He believed in hope, and so, he kept on trying.

"There's so little time to search for the value of my life," rotates San Tong's lips," so little time that I have left. Do you know what I mean, Mansui?" She understands him. Yet, dark meridians continue to make him question the outward slippage of his fate.

"What chance has he at his age?" sighed my siblings and I among ourselves. "Father has too many fires going. He ought to do just one thing and stay focused on it," concluded our congress. This was love bending in sad refrains, singing a dale of pity, for to whittle yourself away in another latitude, in this case Mexico, buys you time but not recovery, not what's been stolen from an immigrant's dream. And betrayal by one's bone folk—by his sisters whom he had raised like daughters—brings a peculiar pain to the human heart.

There's cold dead fear shooting through Father's veins, this I see. But a part of him feels a truth: that the world is moved by unconventional dreams. Father tells himself this is what he must seek to harvest. Psychologically, he accuses himself of not delivering. In reaction to his internal combustion, he attacks Mansui, "You think my leadership hasn't revealed a welcomed path for all in our family to follow—is this what you mean?"

"No, no, you've got me wrong! It's not what you think." Tears blur the corners of Mansui's eyes because she really didn't mean to injure. Her wail, however, stirs an undertow inside a man having been powdered and spread to the far corners of the western plains.

I tell you, Jack, my father's attempt to make an imprint on the world cost him plenty, every ounce of psychic wonder to ply against the oceans of conformity, the path that society feels is reasonable and safe to take. So, it scared me to see my old man storming a separate sea, steering against its bold breakers with a tin spoon. But Father was now free as the tarnished world never had in mind for him. Free to soar his soul beyond December, free to impose upon the living an old humanity: how one's dream needs to be realized—just once—before it exits Time.

The day Mansui departed from our family in the San Fernando Valley, our tribe had gathered around her at the door of a Greyhound bus. After bidding us all farewell, her face poked out an opened window of her Bus, and she mouthed, "This was wonderful, we'll do it again!"

Although Mansui's reunion with Father had not been what she'd expected, she held no grudge toward him. She was accepting of such angles because she was from the old country, too, and because she knew that she was slowly dying. The following year, we received a New Year's greeting card from New York City. It had a painted view of where we would find Mansui: in a place where a water buffalo is fastened forever to the postcard of a dream.

But my siblings and I had missed that clue because we weren't steeped in her tribal tome, we were children of a new generation growing up in the bustling arteries of the West. We absorbed little of the mysteries concerning life in a Chinese village; instead, we noted how Chinatown's cards appeared, well, post-war frugal. But my collapse in that regard was certainly not due to someone's failure to rectify my soul. On the Jue Joe Ranch in the old days Father had tried to teach my siblings and me. One day in grandfather Jue Joe's cabin, I discovered lift-top desks with wooden benches. And laid on top were new schoolbooks in the Chinese language. At each desk a silver inkwell imported from Hong Kong floated you a mossy smell from its wet, silky inkpad. Perched across that inkwell, a Chinese brush with pointed tip beckoned me to walk its tip vertical down mulberry paper. Rigged to one wall I saw a big blackboard roaring squiggles in vertical columns. It was clear to me that Father had hoisted on us a world that would allow my siblings and I to exchange one continent for another, transporting us across geography's vast contours of knowledge.

Our teacher was Reverend Wai Shing Kwok who was the father of my brother Jack's wife Alice. In Sacramento, Reverend Kwok had been a pastor at the Chinese Christian Church and head teacher at the Kwai Wah Chinese language school that served children of immigrants. Now, I remember him floating to us exotic feeling on the blackboard. I remember him staring at our faces blank as beetles because he watched my sister Soo-Jan dip her brush into an inkwell, he watched my other siblings and I follow suit, and we painted faces on our thumbs—finger puppets that waltzed like Balinese dancers.

You ask me, what resulted from our impudence? Make no mistake. You heard Reverend Kwok's wooden pointer slam the blackboard so hard that it snapped the stick in two.

But art is language of a deeper kind, I told my father. He was livid upon learning of our antic. He turned the pockets of his trouser inside out to show me how empty we'd made them become. He moaned, "Money doesn't grow on trees, my children, I've spent bucks to educate you and...."

You get fleeced. That's the human trap. Father flew South of the Border in search of work. Through his correspondence I began to feel a new verve traverse the topography of his vanquished heart. At first, I couldn't put my finger on it, so ambiguous was the thing I detected, but then so undeveloped was I at ruminating on deeper ground. I could imagine, however, a dry cactus wind reducing life to its simplest grain of truth—the way truth begs to be played in the human equation.

The Town of Tulancingo holds a secret. It's where the pine trees smell the sweetest. It's where morning mist rolls back and you see a mountain. And on this mountain, you see a cabin with its door swung open. Through that gap a man steps out just as the rain retracts. He studies peddlers heading on foot down that mountain to a village below.

Burros bundled with packs twice their size, and led by women wrapped in colorful rebozos, trundle toward a market located in Tulancingo's plaza. Sweet-smelling spices drift from their baskets, and feet bound in straw sandals march daily under the grip of Tulancingo's burning sun. For five-hundred years the Town of Tulancingo has refused a glass-and-tower progress. Instead, browsing in and out of earthen huts, chickens and pigs expose their longings. Cats scratch round sheds for a living. And in the distance, there are more shacks, and you hear a child wailing and you watch great lumbering figures stir up cooking smoke.

Tulancingo roosts like a dream one hour north of Mexico City, in the State of Hidalgo. Here, my father discovers a rare embroidery hidden in his soul: he notes that his arms were once strong enough to lift crates filled with asparagus—like iron forklifts—but now, they are the oars of a soul struggling against ominous currents. Still, an old man is brave knowing that he may drown while plying the odds, for resilience is all that he has left.

"FOR STORAGE," scrawls San Tong's pen in Spanish. He underlines the words across his cardboard boxes. Earlier in the day his bags of five-spice peanuts and his bottles of soy sauce flew into those boxes. The Mexican economy had crashed. And San Tong's heart slipped into those boxes too.

In time San Tong unearths fresh hope. He is hired to revitalize a 500-year-old ranch in Tulancingo for a man whose business is leading Mexico City's most powerful labor union; a union that had built Mexico City's subway system. His name? Angel Castro. Señor Castro dreamed of owning a paradise far away from the brutal politics of an urban metropolis. The answer came as a distant ranch set in a peaceful setting in which living creatures knew of freedom.

Castro's ranch? It turned on a squeal, Jack. Chester White pigs, that is. They are intelligent animals. San Tong invents a way to wean newborn piglets at six weeks, instead of fifteen weeks that it usually takes, to move pigs to market in the shortest time. He teaches the raising of hundreds of Chester White pigs to workers on the Tulancingo ranch, and the enterprise proves successful for Angel Castro.

Across the vastness of the ranch a winding path leads San Tong to a remarkable sight. Here, phantasmal rubber plants in shapes unique loom to catch his eyes. The verdant growth reaches for water cascading over boulders to skirt its roots. San Tong's interior notes that these are cactus, cactus of the kind he had read about in headlines splashed across newspapers. For a hushed peyote farm had withdrawn to a small corner of Castro's ranch; once, the entire ranch had been a clandestine enterprise for a previous group of owners.

That night a big stone hearth that San Tong had built in his bedroom lights his dream: on his Guatemalan blanket a figure arises. It's Ping rocking next to his hearth's flames. It's the year San Tong had built this hearth for her, so that she could warm her joints against Winter's arctic nettles shooting down her bones. But Ping is unable to stay in his wilderness, she whispers in his ear. She leaves him and floats on freeways flowing north of the Border; her arthritic fingers beckon him to wander with her on this silent journey.

And there, there at UCLA's sprawling hospital, Ping lay motionless in a quiet room set aside for welfare recipients. She feels a nurse remove her air mask and hears a switch above her headboard flick off and all dreams begin to fade. But San Tong lifts his wife's head and in her moribund hour he pours into her his enormous devotion—heartfelt feelings that she could not reach in their lifetime together, but now, in her peculiar state she possessed.

Through Ping's vanishing tunnels I see my father begin his long journey home to us.

Tulancingo's big ranch holds a pool of speculation. It squats on the rooftop of the 500-year-old hacienda. "Jose" is what the man goes by, and he cleans the pig stalls. On sunny days you'll find Jose squatting on that rooftop. This is where he takes his siestas; that is, after he shoots up. Jose is a remnant from the ranch's earlier chronicle.

"What you on, Jose?" queries San Tong, as he put his face up to Jose's silhouette floating across the roof's pink tiles. To San Tong, this ranch has its strays just as the Jue Joe Ranch once had in the belly of old Van Nuys, California.

"Deadman's acid," pumps the high-pitched craw of Jose. "And you know what? Here's some fire for you, too. I got some—" Jose breaks off as he slides down the roof on a hand-roped ladder.

"That's fire, Jose, you oughta quit," suspends San Tong, squaring Jose in the eye at ground level. His concern grows as he views the stray's infected pupils.

Jose pats his breast pocket for needle and spoon, assuring himself that his only treasures are still with him. He pulls from a pant pocket a paper bag for San Tong.

"Go on and take it," squawks Jose, feeling like an injured hen. He continues, "See for yourself! It ain't noth'in what you think, o.k.?" He shakes his head as if brewing a storm of pity for this old Chinaman and retreats to his temple on the rooftop.

Asleep in the courtyard of the ranch, San Tong's white Volkswagen resembles the rural landscape's character: pockmarks roam round its hide. Dirt powders the lower half of the Volkswagen's torso. The Car's doors squeak from old age if you pull them open, and dust stuck to door hinges flies to cloud your view. But bouncing on the Volkswagen's front seat, now, Jose's paper bag jars open to reveal an enigma. Steering the puffing Car over potholes on a country road, San Tong catches sight of the bag's content. Its a neck. Then a part of glass looms. Tulancingo's rich sunlight reveals to San Tong a bluish-white liquid sloshing round in a small bottle. There's no mistake. This is called "pulque." It is a cactus elixir thick as malt and known by locals as Mexican beer.

"Why, I could make this beer non-alcoholic," triggers San Tong's interior engine. The art of food science takes hold of his sleeping dream; it revs awake to reach high speed. "I can be back in business, and like my father, I'll take the time to grow a thing right." Why be in a panic-hurry? That's when guys my age mess up. And what awaits me but tea with the bone man? I'd burn that invitation if I got one now.

All around him, San Tong notes that a cactus called "Maguey," from which high-grade pulque is extracted, grows wild as far as your eye can see; the plant's grayish-blue tines reach for the sky like upside-down octopuses. Best of this poesy is found in a rural town called "Actopan." And the Town is just a stone's throw away from Tulancingo.

Actopan is an Otomi Indian enclave dwarfed by the Sierra de los Frailes Mountains, which amass northeast of Tulancingo; it is on the way to the silver mines of Pachuca. Looming upward is the Church of San Nicolas built in 1546 by padres of Spanish conquistadors. And near the Falls of St. Francis, San Tong Jue's "Western Advance Corporation" opens with character. Like the sound of the Falls, you hear San Tong's pulque roaring in vats, the content pouring into glass tubes that perculate and that fill the volume of his bottles. He is proud of his labels on the bottles too: mother's milk breast-feeding life into her baby. The non-alcoholic drink begins its distribution on shelves of grocery stores and roadside food stalls.

In time San Tong's "Sun Hing Corporation" opens in Mexico City. It bursts alive in a small house that San Tong had transformed into a factory situated on Villa Obregon, near Reforma Road. This is an old sector filled with old people quietly waiting for new beginnings. Here, San Tong's eyes scan the activities of his new factory. He feels pride that his own hands had designed and delivered mechanized corporals: roasters rotating peanuts to dry them, another to pump damiana tea leaves into teabags. There are boilers bottling soysauce, passion-fruit wine percolating in Alhambra bottles, and champagne bottled in fancy labels. On the factory floor, your ears catch spit gears grinding aloud their language, and fermentation washers vibrating like skilled clothes dryers. Robotic arms package and stamp San Tong's wonders for the Sun Hing Corporation.

Enter Mr Lee who is small in build and who is swirled like a figure eight. He runs a cafe round the corner off Reforma Road. Sundays and a few clients creep into his cafe after church. Otherwise, the cafe on most days boasts a drained appearance. There are wooden booths to provide for a customer's privacy, but the wall's paint is peeling. Tables perched in the open are steadied by newspapers jammed underneath their legs. And the day's menu carries "cafe con leche" as its top billing. Nevertheless, Mr. Lee is overjoyed because adding San Tong's soy sauce and five-spiced peanuts and damiana teabags boosts his café's array of selections. In no time Mr. Lee joins San Tong as a business partner in the Sun Hing Corporation. Overnight, Sun Hing products take Mexico City's supermarkets and its local theaters by storm.

But you never know which way a storm blows, Jack. The pursuit of happiness—like life—is a puzzling affair. Mr Lee floats skyward from a fatal heart attack. And San Tong finds himself, well, the blink of a dream is gone. But not what will always drum quietly in a Chinaman's heart. The family.

For San Tong, that drumbeat lures him towards Central America. To what appears to him like a pop-up village descending upon his heart. By this I mean "Cuilapa," a dusty hamlet located on the western coast of Guatemala.

Cuilapa is where Jue Joe's sister had settled with her husband so many yesteryears ago. The old life tethers San Tong once again to seek his lost family; to seek reunification with the branches of Jue Joe's family now scattered about in the New World.

The white Volkswagen rounds gamely the scrub and up over scarp and down a cleft that would bust a jeep's axle. Wheezing, it knows the importance of its mission and continues to move like an old Mayan warrior through the thick of a Guatemalan jungle. The beauty of the rain forest thrusts up endless heights as wheels of the Car dig the ground. The view reveals to San Tong a reason Jue Joe's sister took a leap, sailing long ago from Sum Gong Village in China, to claim her adventure in this uncharted latitude. Now, to San Tong, her story is an old aunt's trunk filled with silken tales. For the nomad's drumbeat knocks round in all of us. Make no mistake.

Night falls and mist hangs low, and on a stretch of lonely road, the Volkswagen's headlamps show no signs of life. In an instant San Tong's buggy overruns a border crossing in the dark and a motorcycle gives chase. The Guatemalan soldier on the motorcycle blasts a halo of light onto San Tong's bewildered face.

"How much you got?" commands the teenage soldier. He waves his flashlight at San Tong and exclaims again, "How much you got!"

"But I've nothing on me...not much cash...I've only got this car," spills San Tong's concern.

"Senior, you are in liberated territory," commands the teenager. "We are the government." He checks his thought, and rips aloud, "How much money you got?"

"About five hundred," reels San Tong's voice, trying not to count his fears.

"Good, Senior, give me Gringo dollars!" The teen throws San Tong a thumbs up.

"No, no, I've got that much in pesos," amends San Tong. "Pesos," he recounts again.

"Aiy!" exclaims the teenager. "No good, Senior, show me your papers."

On cue San Tong pulls from his shirt pocket a matchbook. He nods a smile and offers, "Will you have a smoke?"

The boy-soldier eyes the matchbook with pesos protruding as if circling a covered wagon. "Gimme seven hundred in Gringo dollars and I let you go."

"But I've only got pesos. Here, take it. Take all of it."

The boy-soldier's eyes waggle with feeling. Then his eyebrows arch as if to cross themselves. In one swift moment, a sound rips from his orifice: "Senior, I arrest you in the name of our Father."

A jail cell. A letter penned in panic. "I need seven hundred dollars in cash—it's urgent!" Father's letter winds its way into our hands in America. The dinero is wired with quickness. Released from his Guatemalan jail, Father continues his journey to find

Jue Joe's sister of yesteryear. Searching hard, Father uncovers descendants of Jue Joe's sister living in Cuilapa. He finds them living in an earthen hut. He finds them poor as church mice. They carry the surname of Jue Joe's Chinese brother-in-law, all right, but features of the descendants appear as native as ever. They speak only Guatemalan, and they dress and look Guatemalan.

CHAPTER 11 – RECONCILIATION

We didn't know that Grammy had died. Corrine and Dorothy had not notified Father of her passing, let alone where they had buried her at Forest Lawn in Glendale, California. Leong Shee was the spirit of our family's heart; she symbolized the continuity of our family split between two continents but holding together in unity. So many times, we had tried to visit Grammy in San Francisco at Corrine's home. So many times, we had tried to contact Grammy by phone as well. But in each instance, we were turned away.

A year earlier Father had gunned his Volkswagen up to San Francisco to see Grammy. Twenty-five years had passed since Dorothy's courtroom brawl, which had changed forever the fate of all our lives. Then, a letter from Corrine to San Tong had changed the tide of sad refrain, so we thought. Grammy was paralyzed from a massive stroke, wrote Corrine. She has no movement from her neck down to her toes.

"Corrine? This is your brother San," voiced Father into a phone. "I—I'm here in San Francisco to see Ma." Cold dead silence floated back to him. "Corrine, are you there?"

"Why San, it's been a long time," replies his sister Corrine. Caught off guard, she can only conjure, "How are you?"

"I'm o.k. I come up to see Ma. She's old, Corrine, and I need to see her before she passes from us." A pause, and he continues, "Thanks for letting me know about Ma."

"San, I—I can't let you see Ma. I just can't and—" Corrine's voice falls hard on him.

"What do you mean?" interrupts San Tong in astonishment. "We're still blood and although we can't change the past, it's time we soften our hearts for Ma's sake. It's been a hard road for my soul to heal, Corrine, but let's honor the good in our family—and that means Ma. I know she wants to see me, Corrine, I can feel her thinking this, and I gotta see her."

"But Dorothy mustn't know that I contacted you, San, she mustn't know. I can't take the chance. She'll be livid. Besides, how can you think that at Ma's age, and in her delicate condition, she could stand the shock?" posed Corrine's gambit. "She will die."

"I hadn't thought about it in that way," responds Father, feeling confused.

"It's better if you don't see Ma because, if Dorothy finds that I've spoken to you, well, you know her wild temper. She wanted to put Ma in an old folk's home. But Lansing and I said, 'No!' We were firm with Dorothy, we told her, 'That's not the Chinese way. It would kill Ma if we did that. What's more, she can't speak English. And there she is with strangers. No, Ma has got to stay with family. You and I will share the burden, Dorothy.' That's what I told her, San."

Corrine could feel her brother's discomfort at the notion of Dorothy parking their mother in an old folk's home. For such behavior is unacceptable in Chinese culture. Since ancient times, the family accepts this honored tradition.

To appease her brother, Corrine throws him a soft landing, "Lansing and I are giving Ma the best of care. You needn't worry, San, she's o.k. We turn Ma over on her bed every day so that she won't get the sores. Where are you staying? I'm coming right over to see you. I want to talk to you, San, I really do. And, and I'll tell Ma that I saw you. She'll be happy about that. So, there's no need for you to see her. It would be too risky for her health."

They met at my apartment by the ocean in San Francisco. Their meeting was as if a hundred years of bittersweet memories on the Jue Joe Ranch had rushed the walls of my apartment.

"...and if Dorothy and I had been older, San," sobbed Corrine between her words, "we would never have done what we did to you. I wouldn't have let Dorothy. I should have stopped her, I know now, but her temper is so mean. I'm afraid of her. Oh San, you must believe me. Do you forgive me?"

Father wept deeply, openly. In a voice torn by the lost seasons of his life. I heard him utter aloud, "Corrine, blood is thicker than water. We are family and that's what is important." This is how Father forgave his sister. To me it felt like a sad enormous sigh.

It was wrenched from deep within his well. This I witnessed. He gave sigh for the waste of lives spent on grievances. In my apartment, I saw two centurions continue down their path of awkward, painful solace. By the end of that tortured meeting, exhaustion weighed all over Father's countenance. On my sofa Father worked old memories across its stains as he watched his sister rise like a brittle antelope—leaning on her walking cane for balance—to vanish through the front door and from our lives. She seemed to feel release from a burden; acquitted of grief caused by years of betrayal by two sisters, which opened upon Father the weight of an endless wound. In that raw moment Father seemed to feel the universe gust ajar in which he glimpsed an essence beyond the din of human corruption. For in that moment, he realized one thing: he came to know what a Chinese family really means. And the moment released in me the will to bless our troubled path, for we are sojourners advancing across the shipyard of chance, we have only our memories. In this case, Father's words to me through letters he had sent from Mexico.

"Dear child,

"Yes, some of them are very good. I went to a seer in China for a reading. I recall that he was good. So accurate were these ancient seers; the skill was passed down from generations. It's not like today. I went to a temple to see him, and he told me about misfortunes that I would be challenged with, and then he predicted my future. Well, the challenges all came true. Now, I am waiting to see if his predictions for the future is correct.

"I have been so busy ever since I came back to Mexico. I was never in the mood to write to anyone. I keep on inventing things to sell and working day and night trying to make a comeback as quickly as I can. I am growing mushroom and just perfected my own method, and last couple of weeks I perfected bottling 'Pulque,' which for hundreds of years big companies and also the Mexican government, off and on trying to bottle it and have imported chemists and technical men to work on this drink and have spended millions of pesos and they all failed. But now I have perfected in bottling it. They all failed because they cannot control the bacteria fermentation. By Lord's help I am able to stop it fermentation in the bottle.

"Now I am ready to put this drink on the market, having labels printed and registering it with the health department.

"Of course I am still continue making soy sauce but have not sold hardly any yet. Still waiting for the government license which I made an application four months ago. Here in Mexico, business progress very slow, waiting for this and waiting for that.

"I have so many irons in the fire one of them should turn out a money maker. I have more faith in the Pulque than anything else and that is what my friends here think too.

"As soon as the company making sales of soy sauce I will start drawing salary. Right now I have about 25 thousand dollars worth of soy sauce all ready bottled and ready to sell the only thing I am waiting for is the license and the labels.

"Keep your chin up keep struggling. We will be all right very soon.

"Love Father

"April 5, 1974"

CHAPTER 12 - LEGACY

Father's legacy is not the one he intended to leave us, but it is the one I most treasure for all that it illuminates about the art of living.

"I tried so hard to make a comeback," floated Father's feelings to me in my apartment in San Francisco. On my sofa he fell to a deep silence. This is because a doctor's news had hit him swiftly. It tore like a river down his great canals. I watched an enormous sadness wash over his face that had no words to express its grief—that the fight for life was over. In its place has come something to take him from this world. We were told that his lung cancer is terminal. He has only months to live.

"I tried so hard to do right," repeated Father, "Lord knows how hard I tried."

His words still sear my soul. I find my interior asking, has Father's life been lived in vain for all the travails that had walked him through the heartbeat of Hell?

No, no, I hear myself answer. A life has not been lived in vain no matter where you're parked on this planet, no matter who you've come to be or have not come to be. In that oddly lit corner of my dream, we arrived together, my tribe and I, to seek a marvel so eternal: what a family really means. In our journey to define what a Chinese American identity means, well, I witnessed a bicultural play of incongruous moves. For the Alien Land Law, spinning from Exclusion Laws aimed at a particular group, was the factor that pushed my tribe over the brink of hard return. Tendering tensions upon one another in misplaced anger we not only ripped apart our seams as a family, but we slammed ourselves into a corridor played by dark illusions. There came Lucifer exploding a flintlock down the legacy of our generations; a wound felt well beyond the arena in which the original combatants—in a Los Angeles courtroom—had stood their ground.

"Why, I'm all the family your father has," said Corrine on the phone to me years after their reconciliation in San Francisco. She continued, "He and Dorothy don't speak, it's terrible! I'm the only one who speaks to everyone in our family. Now, let me talk to your father. I heard that he's very ill and I've just got to talk with him as much as I can."

I wasn't sure if I wanted Father to revisit old heartbreaks again, which I perceived might blow him too soon into the four cardinal winds.

"I just don't know Auntie. I don't think that—"

"You don't have to say it. I know what's on your mind," interrupted Corrine. "Well, I can't change what's happened in the past, nor what you think of me, but that's history now. It doesn't concern you kids. As to your father and I, we've made amends. We still have our differences, but we've made our amends."

I heard my voice explode, "Whether or not Dorothy and you agreed with my father's values, he took responsibility to feed and to clothe and to educate you both. He took that responsibility. He gave you a chance in life that he never had for himself! I know that he worked hard to provide for the family—and that included our family in the Village of Sum Gong too. That's a hell of a burden for one man. And I think it's sad, but I know he loved you both. Why did you and Dorothy fight so hard against his way of showing concern? By this I mean in the way you hurt him. He never denied you money when you wanted it…and, and I don't recall you and Dorothy ever working a nine-to-five job."

"Hey, you hold it," countered a startled Corrine. "Don't talk to me like that! I—"

But I couldn't stop the bitter words that poured from my interior. The power of fester continued to unleash itself. "Dorothy knew that the land meant everything to my father. It was his soul. It's a family's continuity and he felt a duty to maintain it. Dorothy's fight with him—and you took sides with her—was not about money, was it? Both of you married very well, so why did you two choose to destroy my father in the manner that you did? What's more, I think you and Dorothy are smart enough to know that what you've done affects more than just one individual in one generation. We have all been affected. So, where were you when he needed you the most, huh? Where were you, huh?"

I heard no sound emit from Corrine, but a painful long pause. Then in slow motion she rounded aloud three words, "Well, that's life."

Father passed away and his cardboard boxes from Mexico began to arrive one by one at our Northridge home in the San Fernando Valley. One by one, each box brought a new surprise.

"He'd carried our lives with him wherever he moved!" exclaimed my brother Guy in astonishment. He lifted from Father's boxes the photos, cards, letters, that we'd sent to him over the years and that he had carefully bundled with red rubber bands. For down the years of grief we thought our father had abandoned us emotionally. But now we knew it was the strength of Father's love unfolding in those dusty brown boxes, which brought Guy to weep for what in life went unexpressed between father and son. Then I began to understand the anxiety that had taken Father's interior: the fear and shame that we, in our undeveloped wisdom, would belittle him in his hardest hour.

My sister Pingileen and I arrived in the Village of Sum Gong, in China, to gather soil, vegetable seeds, and rice from Jue Joe's front yard. It was for Father because he could not travel to his ancestral home, as is the custom for Chinese at the end of life. We met Cousin Moe and his family for the first time. And we presented him and his family with a tape recording of Father's message to them all. It was powerful, though filled with his coughing between the words and restarts of the recording. Father's words soared round the sitting room of Cousin Moe's house, which connected to Jue Joe's 1903-built compound. And the moment was moving. Even our driver for the day felt touched by Father's words.

Later in the day: "Don't tell'em what we've got, you tell'em what we do"t have," urged Cousin Moe to his mother. Standing at the entrance to Jue Joe's main house, he didn't think we heard him a few feet away. With quickness Cousin Moe listed for my sister and I his concerns:

"...and we need Amercian suit. My mother wants color television, please. Bring my daughter to America, she's of no use here in Sum Gong Village. She find husband in America. You don't know the suffering we went through. You don't know what the Cultural Revolution did to us. And, and we had to burn all the photographs that your father San Tong in Los Angeles had sent to us: photos of the Jue Joe Ranch and so forth. I tell you that we were starving. Hungry the whole time. I tried to contact your father. I'd sent him a letter, but I received no reply. My own bone folk don't pay me no mind." (Blah blah blah.)

A half century of storms broke into the loudest bluster you ever heard. In our 24-hour turnaround trip to China, Cousin Moe had grown into a tall, handsome, middle-aged hornet. There was no trace of the sickly kid that I had heard about who was supposed to emigrate to America in 1937 to become the "adopted son" of my late Uncle San You.

My sister Pingileen pressed into Cousin Moe's palm three-hundred U.S. dollars from Father and his taped message to the family in China. And Moe got a black-and-white portable TV that Pingileen had purchased in a shop on Pedder Street, in Hong Kong, just before we sailed on a ferry up the Pearl River delta and down into Sum Gong Village.

In return, Cousin Moe crammed the history of China into the deep blue sea of us. For the next few hours, he reclaimed our severed halves and made us whole. For he filled us with the lore of our ancestors and culture of Sum Gong Village in one fleeting moment.

A string of firecrackers exploded in front of Jue Joe's main house before we all entered for a viewing. "This is to drive away evil spirits," assured Cousin Moe's craw. "Now, it is safe for us to enter."

And enter Jue Joe's abode we did. The scent of yesteryear flicked about the sitting room. Carved teakwood furniture sat on a tiled floor according to the rules of feng shui. The gray-colored brick walls smelled of the burning of incense. Its pungency lifted us into Leong Shee's kitchen mixed with cooking smells: there was a wok set into a hole on top a brick platform, there was rice straw to burn beneath that wok; below the wok was a bellow to pump, too, keeping a lit fire burning. In Leong Shee's kitchen I saw a chicken meander in and out, searching the floor for what to peck. So natural was the rhythm of village life.

Down musty corridors of Jue Joe's abode—undisturbed for a century—ancient travelers flew eerily past: I felt their robes flutter a noiseless rhyme around me. It was as if these sages compared our likeness to their histories, for I could feel their sigh and stroke upon our purpose. A biography of yesteryears crossed my interior as I ascended stairs so steep in Jue Joe's main house that I felt as though I were scaling the heavens.

On the second floor of Jue Joe's main house I entered an empty bedroom and found the other side of Father. It was here, here that his teakwood dresser stood as the only furniture in that room. The dresser's round eye shot me a reflection of myself. The eye flared at me from between its two support staffs, and each staff fancied a do-jigger set on top of its tip.

I pulled open a drawer of Father's teakwood dresser. Coiled in this drawer and atop Father's school books sat his foot-long braid of hair. When the Qing Dynasty collapsed, and when a New Republic replaced China's face, all males throughout the empire cut off their queues.

"This queue symbolized servitude to Manchu rulers in the Ching Dynasty and was not in keeping with our new ideology. The Revolution freed Chinese from foreign rule and humiliation. We became equal citizens and free to chart our country's own destiny. Sorry I put his pigtail in the drawer, you see, I was thinking—"

"There's no need to explain, Cousin Moe," I heard myself utter. "No need to explain." For I wanted something of Father to remain a mystery inside his teakwood drawer. It was enough that I felt the muse of his yesteryears down my bones.

We left Jue Joe's main house by way of Leong Shee's side door, and I watched Cousin Moe set ablaze another hank of firecrackers to usher forward this following: "May our generations from the West come home—we have such needs."

Well, I can't blame Cousin Moe for his perspective. In the art of living, the human range of experience is so diverse. In the anxious year of 1949, for example, revolution swallowed our family's ancestral lands. China's Civil War had washed away corrupt institutions, but the new owners of the Chinese parcels suspected my family and others who owned land as counter-revolutionary whatnots. Land-use was no longer the Well-Field System that had been practiced in Sum Gong Village since the Song Dynasty. Now, land was tagged for redistribution. So, Western books in Jue Shee's library were also burned. And cadres moved for a time into his library's idle.

I tell you, Jack, in Sum Gong Village little guys who owned a window of wind and water were told that the State now owned loam in free simple, so to speak. But Cousin Moe was adamant that he had saved Jue Joe's main house, and the house of Cousin Sik Loon; *alias,* Chan Lum, which is his birth name. Cousin Moe accomplished this by walking into the "Battle of Yalu," in Korea. This is how he'd emerged as a decorated grunt. He had humped the mountains of Anyang, in northeastern Manchuria, bearing a loaded carbine. He had heroically survived Siberia's ice-winters, and for the next five years—from 1950 onward—he pumped his rifle in cold dead fear at enemy conscripts rushing his line of scrimmage.

Later in the day, Cousin Moe's mother told Pingileen and me of her private pain. It happened during the Great Leap Forward. "Steel," she said. The cold hard truth of steel.

In Sum Gong Village you had to smelt steel. If you lived here in 1958, you had to stoke it and not harvest food from the farm. The first item that she produced? Useless hubcaps made from Leong Shee's iron front gate; the gate that was kept locked to keep the good from vanishing. Only, thirty-million folk slid off the globe in the aftermath of the Chinese famine. In consequence, Moe's mother had to send her only daughter to the Town of Sun Wui to cut it on her own. True. Then, she and her remaining sons stripped the hides off Jue Joe's four lichee trees to eat. No longer could the gramps, now brittle and old, throw their sweet-smelling lichees to satisfy bellies roaring. In finality, Moe's mother was forced to hawk her youngest son, but she couldn't get a fair price for him.

"Things had come to that!" mourned the old biddy. She took my hand in hers, and wailed, "We suffered so much. How we suffered and YOU didn't know."

To Cousin Moe and his family, we in the West could never feel such brutality in the pain of living. We'd forgotten an ancient tenet passed down through ages: it's all for one, and one for all in a Chinese family. This is the premise on which a family survives. Well, Cousin Moe was a teacher of history in Sum Gong Village and, I guess, he felt his duty to explode.

I sat riveted to every turn in Cousin Moe's chronicles, which gave me the clues of a lost account of history now recaptured. Hopefully, it closed a wide gap between us. Hopefully, it bridged two colliding worlds of thought. Only, I couldn't speak a word of Chinese. Instead, I strained myself to understand his complaints in my own way.

The Cultural Revolution of 1966 launched itself with vigor. Cousin Moe saw Jue Joe's flushing toilet—and whatever old or deep in foreign esprit—ripped from the family's experience. Such things had to be discarded. Squads of youth roamed the earth like hungry locusts, burning or smashing what challenged the nation's new thinking. Then, just as abruptly they moved on, leaving the landscape of Sum Gong Village scalped.

When rumors flew from Guangxi Province that there'd been a feast in a remote village of that Province, it sent a chill down the arc of Sum Gong villagers. Starvation had turned some folk to nip at human flesh. Was this paltry gossip? Who knows. In the Pearl River delta, you sensed that only one moral force was binding for folks in the Region: you looked to the North for advancement of narratives; never mind what spills from lessor sources. And folks grousing round the Chinese parcels came to understand this well.

Hen bones. Cousin Moe spit'em on the brick floor. At our farewell luncheon in Jue Joe's compound, the wives had prepared for Pingileen and I a sumptuous meal. I heard Cousin Moe continue to explain the luster of our history, as if we were excavated gems in need of polishing; yes, as if we had lost the essence of our heritage in the long and winding drift down foreign roads.

Afterward, Sum Gong Village began to fade from our vision, as our jitney took the bumps and starts on an old, so very old road back to our hotel in the Town of Sun Wui. I stayed the image of Moe and his family in my mind: the congress waving farewell to my sister and me vanishing from their world. Along the ride, I saw great tendrils of the big canal's mangrove trees—a thousand years of living and still quivering to quench its thirst in the waters of that canal. Strung across my chest was a bandoleer of seeds plucked from Leong Shee's garden that Pingileen had taped beneath my clothing; these seeds felt comforting against Father's oncoming fate. I gave a pat to the treasures bulging from under my clothing because we were determined to beat the U.S. quarantine.

"If you get stopped by the authorities," warned Pingileen, "just tell them you are pregnant. They won't search you."

My plane took flight through puffs of cotton pasted across the sky, and in midair I spilled a few seedlings into my palm and studied their reason for being and I grew sad. Cousin Moe didn't know that Father no longer had the Jue Joe Ranch. I couldn't explain to him in native verse the foreign version of courtroom brawl. This American concept was non-existent in Sum Gong; therefore, the way in which Father's resources dried up and the subsequent absence of his dispatches to family in Sum Gong flew past Moe.

It broke Father's heart that he couldn't make this trip for he teetered on the eve of a cosmic hour. It broke his heart that he couldn't make a comeback in our natural forest for all the seeds he sowed in desperation. But he was a good plant man. He made things grow. And now, Father's descendants rise full throttle to pace the earth with their own undertow of visions, with their own acuity of witness down the arc of the blue ball. Here is a peculiar pivot in all our lives: there are stories to unfold from THE YOU WHO ARE YET TO BE BORN.

When I ride the San Fernando Valley's endless mutations, I feel Father's gong-cries. I feel him turn the Santa Susana winds softly toward the East. I made a U-turn and became its ghostly booty. A vaquero on a mule clutches my soul. My cut-off head chews the leaves fallen from a San Fernando Valley's oak tree. I suppose it doesn't matter who carts away my flesh or in which direction it travels; up or down according to the Christian scale, or sideways or in loops according to other lifts on human ail. But truth be this. I am a part of human verse in the known universe. I feel the spins of life as I robin-hop the Milky Way because I have a duty to explain to you our true story—the story of an immigrant's dream.

EDITOR'S AFTERWORD

My Auntie Soo-Yin is the youngest of my father's sisters. She and I are only eight years apart in age but a generation apart in our respective roles in our family's story. More than twenty years ago my aunt gave her nieces and nephews the gift of a long sprawling unedited first draft of the story of our family . The story captivated me then and has continued to hold me in its spell all these years. I began researching and contributing more detail to our family's story in America and created an internet blog where I collected oral history, photos, poetry, art, film clips and documents from other members of our extended clan (https://juejoeclan.blogspot.com). It has always been my dream to work with my Auntie Soo Yin and to bring her heartfelt memoir of our family to a wider audience. She is a wonderful and gifted storyteller with a unique voice and we have spent many hours writing and talking about the details of the story you have just read. I hope you have enjoyed it as much as I.

Jack Jue Jr. 2023

ABOUT THE AUTHOR

Soo Yin Jue grew up on her family's asparagus ranch in Van Nuys in the San Fernando Valley . The farming operation there was founded by her grandfather who emigrated from China in 1874. She is a second generation Chinese American and both her parents were born in China. She is a retired human resources professional. Throughout her life she has had a keen interest in the history of Chinese in America and the transnational history of her own and other immigrant families. She has been a guest lecturer at high schools and at museums discussing her family's colorful history. This is her first published book.

Made in the USA
Coppell, TX
05 December 2023

25385847R00116